The Haunted Mansion Is Creativity

By Shad Engkilterra

Other books written by Shad Engkilterra:
Disneyland Is Creativity: 25 Tips for Becoming More Creative
Penguinate! The Disney Company: A Wholly Unauthorized Look at the House that Walt Built
Penguinate! Essays and Short Stories: Improving Your Creativity for a Better Life and World
My Life in the Projects: A kid's-eye view to HUD housing in the 1980s
The Pirate Union
Adventures on the Amur #1: The Treasure of Nikolai Nikolaevich
Adventures on the Amur #2: The Curse of the Golden Kopeck
There Are No Penguins in Alaska

Cover image by Antonisa Scott at Transcend Studio
Map illustration by Anton Abela

Join Shad and Jenya at www.patreon.com/penguinate
Follow Shad on Twitter @shadexaminer
Read more at DisneylandIsCreativity.com
Penguinate.com
Penguin8.com

The Haunted Mansion Is Creativity © 2019 by Shad Engkilterra. All Rights Reserved.

All rights reserved. No part of this book may be reproduced in any form or by any electronic or mechanical means including information storage and retrieval systems, without permission in writing from the author. The only exception is by a reviewer, who may quote short excerpts in a review.

Acknowledgements

Thanks to my Patreon Penguinators:

- Drue M. Scott
- Patricia Burleigh
- Rachel O'Brien
- Mary Hawkins
- Celia Wallis

You can join us at www.patreon.com/penguinate for penguins and more creativity.

Thanks to Anton Abela for the great drawing of the path that guests of the Haunted Mansion take during their tour.

Thanks to my cover artist Antonisa Scott at Transcend Studio.

Thanks to my mom who proofreads every book I write.

Thanks to the hundreds of people who made the Haunted Mansion what it is. From the imagineers to the Disneyland Cast Members who work as the hosts, hostesses, and staff at the Haunted Mansion, it's really like Walt Disney said, "You can design and create, and build the most wonderful place in the world. But it takes people to make the dream a reality" (Sources of Insight, Walt Disney Quotes).

Disclaimer

Disneyland, the Walt Disney Company and its subsidiaries have not endorsed this book. No claim to their copyrighted material is maintained or asserted by the author of this book.

"The Haunted Mansion Is Creativity" is in no way authorized by, endorsed by or affiliated with the Walt Disney Company, Inc. or its subsidiaries.

Dedication

To my wife, who has allowed my writing to flourish.

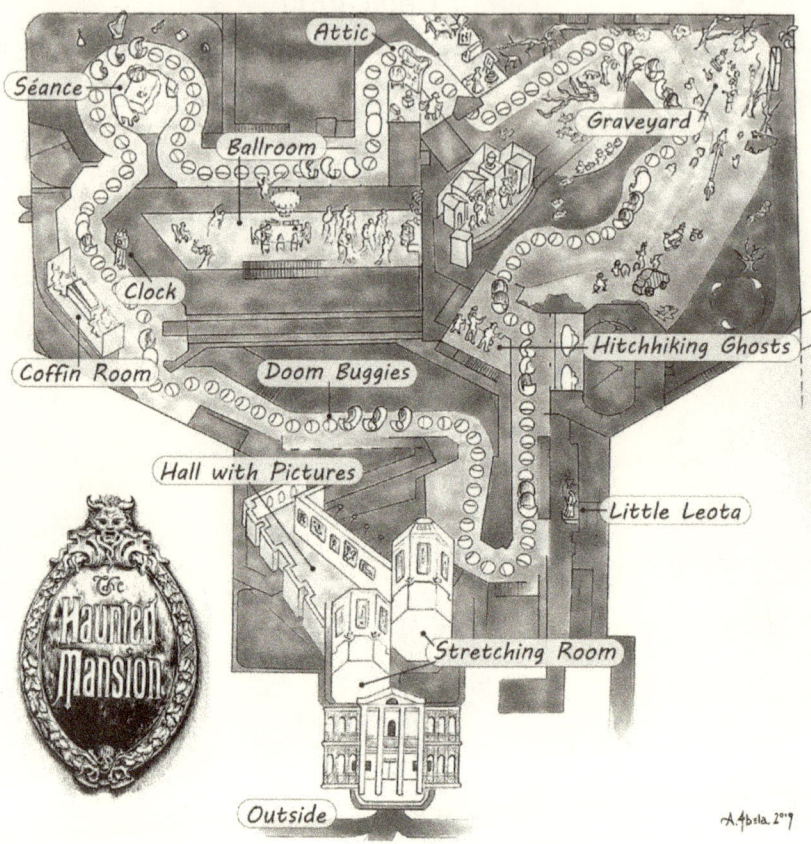

Figure 1: Haunted Mansion Layout by Anton Abela

Table of Contents

Acknowledgements iii
Disclaimer iv
   Foreword ix
Introduction xii
Before Opening Day – Have a Goal 1
   Yale Gracey and Rolly Crump – Write It Down 4
   Gracey and Crump II – Play 7
   Ghost Recruitment – Fill the Well 10
   Delayed Development – Keep Learning 14
The Haunted Mansion: The Tour 18
   Outside the Mansion – Expect Rejection 18
   The Grounds – Get Comfortable 22
   The Hearse – Take a Risk 25
   The Pet Cemetery – Carry the Process Further 27
   The Butler and Maid – Find and Be a Mentor 31
   The Foyer – Practice 34
   The Stretching Room – Stretch Your Imagination 38
   The Portrait Gallery – Embrace Change 43
   The Busts – Change Your Perspective 46
   A Limbo of Boundless Mist – Tolerate Ambiguity 48

The Doom Buggies – Keep the Ideas Flowing	51
The Endless Hallway – Be Curious	56
The Conservatory – Believe You Can	59
The Corridor of Doors – Have Courage	62
The Clock – Make Time	65
The Séance Circle – Synergy	69
The Grand Hall – A Stimulating Environment	72
Pepper's Ghost – Making Something Old New Again	77
The Attic – Tell Your Story	80
Out of the Attic – Failure and Mistakes	85
The Graveyard – At the Intersection	88
Grim Grinning Ghosts – Teamwork	93
The Crypt – Travel	96
The Exit – Humor	99
Afterword: Memories from Mom	102
Practical Guide to Improving Creativity	104
Disneyland Glossary and Other Terms	115
The Characters of the Haunted Mansion	118
The Creators of the Haunted Mansion	121
Resources and Bibliography	125
About the Author	131

Foreword
By Darren Lamb

Shortly after my daughter Rowan turned five, she suffered a severe stoke that drastically impacted the left side of her body. Her left arm wouldn't work at all, her left leg would barely move under her own will power, and she basically had to learn to stand and walk all over again. Doctors couldn't explain why it happened, and as a family, we were distraught. There was nothing we could do to 'fix' the situation. All we could do was help Rowan with her physical therapy and hope that another stroke wasn't looming in her future.

Like many Americans who have faced family struggles, we were looking for some type of emotional Band-Aid for what we were all going through, and we figured "the Happiest Place on Earth," could provide my daughter with some much-needed fun time.

We had to rent a stroller because Rowan was still struggling with walking, and I tried to ignore the judgmental looks I received for pushing around an older child in a stroller. Rowan would try to walk whenever she could though, and most of the time, I just carried her.

Early in the day, we found ourselves in New Orleans Square, and I was excited to go on my favorite ride in the park: The Haunted Mansion. My daughter was nervous because she didn't like scary things, but after some convincing, she decided to try.

"Welcome foolish mortals," the ghost host said as we entered the circular, stretchy room. I could tell Rowan was nervous, but I tried to joke with her about the silly puns, like making our way to the dead center of the room, and Rowan seemed to take it in stride.

As the room 'stretched' to lower us down to the ride's loading platform, the ghost narrator told us about the "dismaying observation: this chamber has no windows or doors...which offers you this chilling challenge: to find a way out! Of course, there's always my way." Lightning flashes, someone screams, and a body hangs lifeless from the rafters, gently swinging back and forth.

My daughter naturally asked why a man was hanging up there. Now, I was already feeling bad for perhaps taking her on a scary ride that was pushing the boundaries of age appropriateness, so I decided not to tell her the truth, but rather go with something light and fun. "The Hunchback of Notre Dame" had just come out and was currently in the rotation of movies she was watching, so I told her the man was Quasimodo, ringing the bells. She nodded, and we proceeded through the ride. When it was over, she was fine but said she would rather not go on the ride again (this, of course, would change once she got older, especially when they add "The Nightmare Before Christmas" stuff in there during the holiday season).

Later that night, we were in the California Adventure side of the park watching Buzz, Woody, and several of the other Pixar Characters in the Pixar Parade; I was holding her on my shoulders so she could better see the parade when she gently tapped me on the head and whispered, "Dad, I don't think that was Quasimodo".

To this day, some 20 years later, she still jokingly teases me about lying to her that day.

Author Darren Lamb is a Disney enthusiast. He collaborated with his daughter, Rowan, on "The Worst Buddhist", a children's book about dealing with difficult emotions and meditation. Darren writes adult fiction and non-fiction with Buddhist overtones and a decidedly geeky bent. His books include the Sea of Sin series, "Rebirth: A Zombie Tale" and "Ronin Buddhism."

Introduction

While I would like to begin this introduction with the Ghost Host's famous opening line from the Haunted Mansion, I don't want to be too repetitive or cliché, so I'm going to leave it until he decides to materialize later in the book.

I have loved the Haunted Mansion for as long as I can remember. When I went to Disneyland some time before graduating from high school with an older friend and without my mom or my sister, we spent one evening going through the attraction again and again so we could learn the spiel from beginning to end. The swinging wake always mystifies me with wonder, even though I know the technology is an effect called "Pepper's Ghost" from the 19th century.

The stretching gallery, the pictures in the corridor (before Disney changed them) leading up to the Doom Buggies, the busts that watch your every move, the deep rich voice of the Ghost Host, the floating head of Madame Leota, the hitchhiking ghosts who must've followed me home at least 100 times, the caretaker that's more afraid than we are, the eternal hall... Sorry, I've gotten carried away with the spirit of the Haunted Mansion. In short, I love it all.

The Haunted Mansion is my favorite attraction at the park, and hopefully, it's yours, too. (That's from a different attraction, isn't it?)

The information on the following pages is arranged in the form of a tour, but not just any tour, it's the tour of the Haunted Mansion. I combine a detailed account of the attraction, describing in detail every step and every scene as of 2018, with stories from its history, starting from before the Haunted Mansion opened in 1969 and continuing until its current incarnation. These tales and the features of the attraction are used to illustrate principles of creativity found in academic literature and interviews with people who are engaged in creative careers or are acknowledged as creative.

By combining the Haunted Mansion and its history with principles of creativity, you'll be able to better grasp how to be more creative because you are creative. You may not have the key to unlock that creativity, and this skeleton key is my gift to you. If you can believe in the ghosts of the Haunted Mansion, you can harness your own natural creativity and enhance it.

With creativity you will not only look alive, you'll feel alive. So, leave your death certificate for your future application to the retirement home for ghosts and follow me into the vast and boundless limbo of discovering and improving your creative talents.

Before Opening Day – Have a Goal

Walt Disney's ideas for a park had always included a haunted house. In 1951, Harper Goff envisioned a church, a graveyard and a haunted house on a hill for the proposed park across from the Disney Studios in Burbank. According to Jason Surrell, Goff was the first imagineer and his 1951 drawing was the first drawing of a haunted house for a Disney park (2015, p. 11- 12). Disney's idea for a theme park outgrew the Burbank location, and he went to Anaheim to find a location for what is now known as Disneyland. In Marvin Davis' concepts for the park, a haunted house was planned for a side street off of Main Street, U.S.A. The idea died as other lands were planned for the area where the side street was to be located. None of those other lands made the cut, either, and in 1955, Disneyland opened without a haunted house.

In 1957, Walt Disney resurrected the idea of a haunted house and assigned Ken Anderson to come up with a story. It would be set in New Orleans Square.

"The creator sets him- or herself problems in order to think" (Gruber and Wallace, p. 108). Anderson came up with several different storylines for the mansion, and started off as the only imagineer assigned to the project. Anderson had his goal set for him by Disney. To achieve that goal, Anderson had to come up with the route to get there. Gruber said "in order to make grand goals attainable, the creator must invent and pursue subgoals" (Lavery, 2014, p. 24).

Without a creative goal, you could wind up endlessly coming up with new ideas for different problems and in different disciplines. The goal provides you with restrictions or constraints. These "constraints provide opportunity" (Nye, 2017, p. viii). "Constraints help you figure out what to not do and, more to the point, what ideas to leave out" (Nye, 2017, p. 116). "Each constraint inspires a new solution to draw on for the future" (Nye, 2017, p. 128). "Innovators embrace constraints," said U.S. Department of State Director of the Office of e-Diplomacy Richard Broly (McDonald, 2013, p. 48).

"Resource constraints mean that people go and find interesting solutions to work around all those constraints," said Gustav Praeklt, founder of the Praekelt Group and Praekelt Foundation (McDonald, 2013, p. 73). Restrictions, either self-imposed or generated from outside the creator, are the key to taking creative ideas into the real world as innovations.

"Everyone needs goals" (Questlove and Greenman, 2018, p. 32).

The goal also allows you to focus your attention on something and to bring your ideas to life. That doesn't mean you should ignore a great idea if the door should open to one. It just means you need to make sure that you're actually creating in addition to coming up with new ideas. Csikszentmihalyi says that having a goal gives you something to look toward. Creative people have goals that they believe are meaningful (2013, p. 349). Find a goal that is meaningful for you.

Yale Gracey and Rolly Crump – Write It Down

In 1959, Disney recruited Rolly Crump and Yale Gracey to work on ideas for the Haunted Mansion. Rolly Crump and Yale Gracey "dug out everything that had been developed for the haunted house up to that time and used it as a spring board for new concepts and special effects" (Surrell, 2015, p. 18).

They gathered everything that had been thought of, and recorded through notes and drawings, and started adding to it and culling from it. This was only possible because the records of Ken Anderson's ideas and story treatments of the Haunted Mansion had been saved and passed on.

"Most creative people keep a diary, or notes, or lab records to make their experiences more concrete and enduring" (Csikszentmihalyi, 2013, p. 347). According to Brightidea cofounder Vincent Carbone, Thomas Edison tracked his ideas on index cards that he could consult and cross-reference (as cited in McDonald, 2013, p. 28). In "Innovators," Walter Isaacson notes that Charles Babbage used "scribbling books" to make notes (2014, p.23).

Keeping notes is important enough that Leonardo da Vinci wrote his backwards. Charles Darwin kept a notebook on his trip around the world. Albert Einstein "usually had a notebook in his pocket" (Policastro and Gardner, 1999, p. 214). It is equally important for you to keep a journal that has the ideas that you come up with. Then if you don't have time to deal with the idea immediately, you have it captured for later.

"A story idea is liable to come flitting into the mind at any moment of the day, and if I don't make note of it at once, right then and there, it will be gone forever" said author Roald Dahl (2013, p. 212). That's true for most creators, especially when they are in the flow of generating ideas.

Takeo Higuchi (2014) recommends keeping an idea journal for his Idea Marathon. He says that by keeping the journal, which includes numbering ideas in order and a point system, you are telling your brain that having ideas is important. He recommends coming up with at least three new ideas a day though recognizes that time constraints may lead to only have one idea. By collecting your ideas in a journal, or set of journals, you'll be able to come back to them.

Imagineer Don Hahn (2011) suggests that the journal be kept private. This will keep the journal honest and allow you to record all of the ideas that you may have without worry about being judged for having them. Hahn says that people like chefs, doctors and scientists, keep notes in their professional life. Journals don't have to limited to words only; you can keep a journal using collage techniques and drawings.

"Maintaining a journal with both written and visual thoughts is a long-standing tradition among artists," says author Lisa Congdon (2014, p. 21). You don't have to be an artist to take advantage of the power of a journal. Writing down your thoughts, emotions and ideas can help you work through problems of all kinds, including creative blocks and a lack of inspiration.

"Notes really help me. If you have an idea, just write it down," says S.T.E.A.M. writer Ashley Peschel (2015).

Walt Disney "kept a notepad by his bed. When he woke up in the middle of the night with an idea, he would write it down and go back to sleep" (Bob Thomas as cited in Williams and Denney, 2014, p. 229). Having a place where you can gather together your ideas will help you keep those ideas flowing and allow you to go back and work on those ideas that seem the most promising, even if you're too busy to do anything more than note them when they appear.

The Walt Disney Company has a long history of never throwing any ideas away. By keeping track of these ideas and revisiting them from time to time, old projects are completed or become new projects. The idea for a movie based on Hans Christian Anderson's "The Snow Queen" started in 1943. It didn't result in a film until 2013's "Frozen."

Dick Irvine said "You never know when you start down another road that one of these ideas won't come back and be used in a different manner" (Kurtti, 2008, p. 22). Having a record of the ideas is the only way to make sure they don't get lost.

Gracey and Crump II – Play

According to Marty Sklar, Walt Disney allowed Yale Gracey and Rolly Crump to "play," freeing them up to experiment (Surrell, 2015, p. 4). They had time, space and notes to play with. "Walt told Yale Gracey and Rolly Crump to play and, you know, to them that was magic because playing meant they could do anything they wanted, and you know, within the confines of the story ideas" (Aitken, 2007A).

And play they did. They had handstand-walking contests, threw a frisbee around, and had yo-yo contests (Kurtti, 2008, p. 67-68).

"We sat around and read ghost stories... We started doing these little models to show Walt.... We did all sorts of crazy stuff. We just played around with all kinds of stuff in that big room..." said Crump (Surrell, 2015, p. 18).

Studies show that "a playful approach to the task at hand increases the likelihood of producing creative results" (Policastro and Gardner, 1999, p. 216). If you've ever seen children at play, you know they make up a lot of the rules as they go. They also use their imaginations without reserve. When children are acting as if they were adults in different roles are envisioning how life would be if they actually took on that role. They are also taking on their anxieties and fears while having fun doing so. From tea time with dollies to playing army and house, children are using their imagination to create situations that they may experience later in life. Children use unstructured role playing to fly like their favorite superheroes, become strong like their heroes, and to find out what life as mommy, daddy, doctor, veterinarian, and other professional and social roles is like. Children who play more become more creative adults (Gentry, 2015).

As they grow, play can take them further into the realm of imagination and fantasy. Role-playing games like "Dungeons and Dragons" allow older children (and adults) to explore different subject matter related to the real world while playing with it in an imaginary arena. History provides the idea of weapons and castle protection. Architecture sets the scene in town. Mythology forms a core of game-playing. Art and math are used to express characters. Highly participative games that don't have a set scenery require that imagination become a part of them.

Play that allows the participant to take on a different role, also allows the player to see things from a different perspective. It is this different perspective that may have the most profound impact on creativity. Imagining being another person or at a different job is at the core of being able to experience what others may think or feel; it will also improve creativity because how things are seen is a large part of changing outlooks.

In adults, play can invoke the freedom of childhood and limit inhibitions, which increases creative output. If you're too serious or you're unwilling to play with ideas and solutions, it's much more difficult to find the elasticity of mind that creativity requires. "Have a playful attitude… If you don't have a playful attitude then you'll never become more creative," says R2D2 builder Tony Dyson (2015). Playing frees you to do things you may not ordinarily consider.

"We were like a couple of kids just doing whatever we wanted to," said Rolly Crump (Surrell, 2015, p. 18) Sometimes, it helps to play with something other than the project or problem you're currently working on. If you feel like "playful spooks have interrupted our tour," consider what the ghosts are doing and follow their lead.

Ghost Recruitment – Fill the Well

In 1962, the foundation for the Haunted Mansion was literally laid, and when it was finished in 1963, it still lacked occupants. Marty Sklar wrote up an announcement that was placed outside of the mansion announcing space available for the dearly departed:

> Notice! All ghosts and restless spirits\ Post-lifetime leases are now available in this\ Haunted Mansion\ don't be left out in the sunshine! Enjoy active retirement in this country club atmosphere - the fashionable address for famous ghosts, ghosts trying to make a name for themselves... and ghosts afraid to live by themselves! Leases include License to scare the daylights out of guests visiting the Portrait Gallery, Museum of the Supernatural, graveyard and other happy haunting grounds. for reservations send resume of past experience to:\ Ghost Relations Dept. Disneyland\ Please! Do not apply in person (Surrell, 2015, p. 20).

Just like the Haunted Mansion needed to be filled with ghosts, you need to be filled with information that you can create from. Your creative well needs to be filled and refilled. It needs a flow of information, some of it related to the project you're doing at the moment, and some of it unrelated.

"Crump and Gracey ended up spending lots of time together researching the horror media of the day, which included seeing monster movie matinees" (Baham, 2014, p. 33).

As a creator, you have a certain amount of energy that you can expend. It's different for everyone, so you need to find your own limit. This energy is often described as coming from a well. If you keep drawing from the well nonstop, it will run dry. You may hit a block, you may run out of ideas, you may feel too tired to continue working on your project or problem. This well needs to be refilled from time to time.

Artist Dean Fenech describes his well as a cup. "You need to fill the cup… either with experiences or with other forms of entertainment that rejuvenates you to give you more motivation," (2015).

Depending on the depth of the well that you need to fill, you may be able to do something as easy as taking a short walk around the neighborhood or through a park. Walking is a time-honored tradition among writers and other creative people. It gets the real-life juices flowing while allowing you to concentrate on something other than the problem at hand and nothing at all.

Yoga is another form of getting the body moving that can help creatively because it comes with the added element of meditation. Taking your focus off the problem and allowing your mind to fix on your breath is a great way for some to reconnect with and replenish their inner well of energy, especially as it becomes a part of a daily habit.

Find creative inspiration in writing. If your creative activity is in something other than writing, you may find beneficial to write without any destination. While writers are able to benefit from freestyle writing, in which they write down any words that come to mind without regard as to how they fit together or what the grammar is supposed to be to connect, it is even more beneficial for painters, sculpture, mathematicians, and scientists. Just giving yourself the opportunity to free associate in written form can help you regain the traction you need to fill your well.

Reading is also a good way to get inspired, but you have to do it with an eye toward thinking deeply. Check out an article on the Internet about something interesting and sit with it. Read it carefully and avoid skimming. Think about it. What's the author saying? Is it different from what he or she is trying to say? What does it mean for you? How can you bring it to bear in your life? Find questions to ask about it, but don't research the answers until you've come up with some ideas of your own.

Find someone else who's creative and enjoy their company. You don't have to talk about your well or replenishing it. You don't have to talk about what you're working on. Simply talk about whatever is interesting for both of you. And remember to listen without preparing what you're going to say next. It's the interaction that's important.

At some point, you may need to allow yourself to do nothing. No TV, no Netflix, No phone… Just sit and relax enjoying the moment. For those who depend on their creativity to make a living, this is one of the hardest things to do. However, by taking a day off, you'll be able to come back stronger than before, and your creative well will be ready to serve you again.

Fortunately, you don't have to fill your well with the body of a wife who has found out that you're secretly a notorious pirate, like one of the Haunted Mansion stories proposed. That would be illegal and immoral even if you're a horror writer. You just need to find what activities help keep you mentally and creatively healthy.

Delayed Development – Keep Learning

The development of the Haunted Mansion was put on hold as Walt Disney committed to building attractions for the New York World's Fair in 1964 and 1965. After the fair, Marc Davis and Claude Coats were assigned to the development of the Haunted Mansion, and X. Atencio joined them.

The World's Fair allowed the imagineers to develop new technologies they could use for Disneyland. They kept learning, and it helped improve the ideas for the Haunted Mansion. Knowledge is important for creativity, so much so that Weisberg (1999) has said that "it may not be necessary to assume that creative individuals differ from the noncreative in any significant way, except for the knowledge they possess" (p. 248).

Because creativity is the combining of two things in a new way, learning is an important way to keep new, high-quality information in your internal creative process. The process of learning should continue throughout life, especially given the fast pace at which life and technology are currently changing.

Learning is taking in new information that changes behavior. Knowing where to find information and how to use the Internet to look it up is important; however, it should not take the place of remembering information. In moments of creativity, you do not want to have to the handicap of having to look something up. Instead, you want to be able to access the information and combine it with no intermediary and no other distractions.

While it's important to continue learning in your chosen field. You will want to explore other fields as well. At the beginning of your journey into a new field, you might want to check out some children's books on the subject. Children's books are good at making complicated information and subjects accessible while eliminating a lot of the bias that may be found in literature targeted at adults. Having a child's understanding of the subject can help you play with the information. Once you have a handle on the subject at a basic level, you can find more scholarly information. If children's books aren't your thing, magazines and newspapers often provide good information in digestible amounts.

There are many different ways to learn. Classes at the community college or local university may drive formal learning. Many libraries and museums have informative programs that are less formal but can still drive the learning process. Bookstores are also a great place to find new information. They often invite authors to talk about their new books. Reading books, magazines, and articles from trusted sources are also good ways to increase learning and expand horizons. Documentaries can also increase the amount of information available to you for creative endeavors.

People learn in different ways, and you probably know the best way to remember new information and incorporate it into your life. Use what you know about your learning style and adopt habits that help feed new information into your system. If you have to write things down in order to learn them, consider starting a blog. If you need someone to hold you accountable, consider joining a book group that reads outside of your normal genre. If you need to move to learn, don't be afraid to add that to your learning time. As long as you aren't in school, you can adopt the habits that best suit you!

Walt Disney continued learning throughout his life. He learned animation and storytelling through doing. He learned how to make miniatures. In 1949, he went to the studios machine shop and learned to use the tools to build a steam locomotive, the Lilly Belle, with the help of Roger Broggie (Kurtti, 2008, p. 95). When Walt became interested in making something new, he learned everything he could about it. In the planning of EPCOT, he learned as much as he could about designing living communities that were good for the people in them and the world. Walt's learning came from his curiosity and his desire to do things.

"The more you learn, the more there is to enjoy about the world" (Nye, 2017, p. 33).

Work on the Haunted Mansion stalled again when Walt Disney died in 1966. There were two factions, one sided with Davis and wanted a humorous attraction and the other sided with Coats who wanted a scarier attraction, Walt wasn't there to break the tie. Dick Irvine took over supervision of the project, and Davis was able to sway him toward comedy. Atencio wrote the script and song, the attraction became a ride-through not a walk-through. On August 9, 1969, the Haunted Mansion was open to the public becoming an instant classic.

    As long as you've gotten this far, as they say, look alive. There's only turning the page now, and we'll begin our little tour.

The Haunted Mansion: The Tour

Outside the Mansion – Expect Rejection

The red brick and green wrought iron fence with arrowheads at the top of it surround the white Antebellum-style manor. Ivy crawls up the iron as if it's trying to get out of the yard. The house is three stories tall with a cupola and a weather vane in the shape of a ship, which marks its owner as a sea-farer or someone who made his living from the ocean. The smell of cinnamon, sugar and dough from a nearby churro cart permeates the air. You walk up to the gateway with two red brick columns -- one on either side.

The two columns feature a shield in the same color as the green wrought iron fencing and shaped like a wreath. At the top of the wreath is a screaming demon with horns; at the bottom of the shield is a skull above a bow. In the middle is written "The Haunted Mansion." Above each of the columns is a large black lantern to provide light when the sun goes down.

The gate is open and beckons you forward. A host and hostess dressed in green, purple and black greets you and checks your ticket: FASTPASS to the right, others to the left. You have a slightly uneasy feeling though you're not exactly sure why. The concrete walkway is white and clean. Grass on the hill to your left is freshly mowed. Every so often the concrete path is crossed with bricks.

"Everyone expects a residence for ghosts to be run-down. But Walt was always looking for the unexpected," said Claude Coats (Gennawey, 2014, p. 180).

His imagineers didn't really understand what Walt was trying to do with the Haunted Mansion. When Ken Anderson came up with his concept in 1957, it was a moldy, rotting building. Walt didn't like it. Harriet Burns drew up three different variations -- two of which were typical haunted house style. They were decrepit and decaying. The third, which the imagineers pushed to the back, was a clean mansion without a blemish. Walt picked the clean version every time.

Walt was lucky because he could overcome rejections through the respect his imagineers had for him and through his authority in the organization. He was the boss. He also had an amazingly successful track record for developing popular and successful entertainment, and he respected that his imagineers would give him a choice.

Ken Anderson came up with a storyline involving pirate and bride. Another storyline featured the headless horseman. A third storyline included Walt Disney himself. While shades of the first story can still be seen in the Haunted Mansion, they were originally rejected as not quite right.

"It's probably safe to assume that despite [Ken] Anderson's best efforts throughout 1957 and into 1958, his ghost house proposals simply didn't capture whatever it was that Walt Disney was looking for. Still, Anderson's seminal work on the ghost house remains instructive to many imagineers today" (Baham, 2014, p. 27).

Without Ken's work, the Haunted Mansion would be drastically different than what exists today. "Ken Anderson is one of the biggest unsung heroes of the Haunted Mansion," said Surrell (Baham, 2014, p. 27).

In 1964, Rolly Crump wanted to do something different, he felt clichés weren't going to cut it for a Haunted Mansion at Disneyland. He wanted to use the human anatomy as the basis for architecture, and came up with ideas like a melting wax man and a chair that could interact with guests. While Walt liked Rolly Crump's ideas that were to be included in the Museum of the Weird, ultimately the museum never came to life. Rejection of these ideas wasn't a commentary on Anderson or Crump. They just weren't right for what Walt, and later, what the Walt Disney Company wanted for the Haunted Mansion.

"Rejection has value" (Ashton, 2015, p. 82). Some ideas are rejected because they are new. However, some ideas are rejected because they don't work or are actually dangerous. Most people are trying to be helpful or protect something when they reject an idea. Creators should take the rejections seriously but not personally. If the creator knows the rejection of the idea is unfounded, he or she should work to prove that the idea will work. However, that means accepting rejections when the concerns are valid. "Creators must expect rejection" (Ashton, 2015, p. 88).

Of course, if you're going to get rejected (and you will), you want to know how to deal with it. When you get rejected, acknowledge your feelings and be kind to yourself. Rejection isn't a reflection on you or your work. It is often a reflection of fear of change or the unknown. If your creativity leads to something ground-breaking, people are going to reject it. If your creating art, you may not be able to find a place to publish it or display it.

Take what you can from the rejection. Allow it to motivate you to do more and to do better. If you know the reason for the rejection, assess its validity. If the reason behind the rejection is a valid criticism, take it and change your innovation for the better. Be sure to consider any criticisms honestly.

The Grounds – Get Comfortable

The home and the grounds are immaculate and inviting. Walt Disney didn't want his mansion to be crumbling and decaying. He wanted everything in his park to be clean and beautiful. He wanted a place where people could be comfortable. He was building something that was different from anything that came before it.

"We'll take care of the outside and let the ghosts take care of the inside," said Walt Disney (Surrell, 2015, p. 13). Walt wanted people to be comfortable in his park. That included being comfortable near the Mansion, even for the guests who weren't going in.

Of course, the smell of a freshly-baked churro increases the amount of comfort guests feel. Bread, cinnamon, sugar and sometimes, special flavors… Who can resist this doughy comfort food?

In organizational creativity, employees must be free to make mistakes and fail, and they must be comfortable knowing that their jobs won't be in danger if an idea doesn't pan out.

CEO of EyeNetra.com David Schafran says the process for creating ideas needs to be designed so people will "let down their guard and start opening up in a way they normally wouldn't do" (McDonald, 2013, p. 108). In other words, they need to be comfortable.

Walt Disney encouraged his imagineers to innovate by giving them a safe place to do so. While he didn't tolerate people, who told him why something couldn't be done, he was generally gentle when asking his imagineers to make changes. He wouldn't criticize. Instead, he would ask if the imagineer could try something else. His team new that it was okay to experiment and come up with ideas as long as they were all headed in the relatively same direction.

As individuals, people are able to harness their creativity better in places where they feel comfortable. Author Ray Bradbury's office as featured at the opening of "Ray Bradbury Theatre" is one example of a place where a creative person felt comfortable creating. Rod Serling used the family Cayuga Lake property as a place to get away from the stress of Hollywood and a place where he could create.

Zern Liew says "You can't be truly innovative unless you have a psychologically safe place" (McDonald, 2013, p. 185). Creativity is a big enough risk without worrying if its going to cost you a job, family, friends, or other parts of your life. Creating a safe place for yourself is essential to becoming more creative.

"When you feel safe and secure in your position, you can be an engaged and curious explorer, taking risks and being creative" (Kashdan, 2009, p. 116). Once you know your in a safe, comfortable place, you can step outside of box and become uncomfortable on your own terms.

Creating your own safe place to create may mean setting aside a room in the house. It may mean having a chest where you keep your projects to work on. It may be as simple as getting your family to support your decision to do something differently and gaining the self-image that allows you to recognize that you are creative. Whatever it takes, find a way to become comfortable with yourself and your space to become more creative.

The Hearse – Take a Risk

You go forward to the white hearse with the horse trappings pulling it. It couldn't be a ghost horse, or could it? The hearse is falsely rumored to have been the same one that carried Brigham Young's body. Inside the hearse are candles, Easter lilies and an announcement that reservations are being accepted at the Ghost Relations department. However, applicants should not apply in person. This may be the first intimation that your experience is undergoing a disquieting metamorphosis. The hearse sits in a courtyard where red brick makes a circle around the center of the white concrete and seemingly extends to each of the points of the compass.

The mansion looks inviting enough, but a hearse out front could be a harbinger of death or something sinister. Continue on, and you're taking the risk that you will see ghosts and possibly be haunted. If you're like most people, it's an easy risk to take. After all, you've come this far through the Happiest Place on Earth. You've been made to feel comfortable with the well-kept grounds, and the Haunted Mansion is an attraction that's been around for decades. As far as you know, no one has died on the ride despite what rumors may have existed in the early '60s.

"Risk taking, along with its accompanying misgivings, forms an inherent part of the creative process" (Ealy, 1995, p. 204).

According to Co-Founder of the Singularity University Salim Ismail, "the biggest imperative for innovation is the willingness to take risk(s). If you want to make a big impact, you have to take a big risk" (McDonald, 2013, p. 131).

Nye encourages people to take the risk and do their best work (2017, p. 131).

When Walt Disney assigned X. Atencio to write the script for the Pirates of the Caribbean, Walt was taking a risk. Atencio had never written a song before, so when he accepted the challenge, he was taking a risk, too, though people said Walt was tolerant of mistakes and failures. Walt and Atencio engaged in the same type of risk behavior when Walt assigned Atencio to write the lyrics to the song Atencio had suggested for the attraction and team with George Bruns for the music. It worked out on both accounts, and Atencio went on to write the script and lyrics for the Haunted Mansion.

In creativity, taking a risk is a little harder. New ideas don't always work out. Prototypes fail. Worse, in some places, being creative is unacceptable, even if there are open statements from the CEO saying otherwise. But, if you want to be creative, you need to take the risk.

Sometimes, you need to get used to risk-taking. Start with something small that you find risky. That may be eating at a new restaurant or trying a new color out on your bedroom walls. Maybe it's trying a new activity like a public art class or riding a bike. Start with a small risk, and then do the next small risk and keep improving your risk tolerance. When you fail, don't take it personally. Instead, realize that it's all part of the process to becoming a better, more creative you.

The Pet Cemetery – Carry the Process Further

The path curves around the hill with the grass and goes by a pet cemetery. A sculpted, nameless cat stands atop a pedestal surrounded by grave markers for five birds. Farther on, a sculpted Freddie the Bat hangs upside down from the point of his head stone and right side up at the foot of it. He died in 1847, and the upside-down epitaph reads "We'll miss you." An unnamed rabbit sits in front of Freddie. Next to the rabbit is Old Flybait, a toad who croaked on August 9, 1869, exactly 100 years before the opening of the Haunted Mansion as it stands now. Behind the toad is Rosie the Pig. "She was a poor little pig, but she bought the farm" in 1849. An urn filled with green plants is placed in the middle of the four gravestones.

Continuing on, an urn with red flowers demarcates a different section of the cemetery. Buddy the Dog, who was a "friend to the end." To the right behind Buddy is a marker for Fifi, who is a poodle. Mounted on the wall behind the dogs are markers for other animals. A long, squiggly marker reads "Here lies my snake whose fatal mistake was frightening the gardener who carried a rake." Above the snake on the left is a marker for a rat without a name, "whom I loved, now he resides in realms above." In the middle is Long-Legged Jeb, a spider, who "Got tangled up in his very own web." On the right is a set of fishbones that died on October 10, 1867. On the column at the end of the wall is another marker that simply reads "July 11, 1864."

Under the tree is an unnamed squirrel. As the path makes a sharper right turn, Lilac the Skunk finishes the collection of pets. She was "long on curiosity, short on common scents."

According to Surrell (2015) and supported by the D23 website, Kim Irvine, daughter of Leota Toombs, found garden statuary in the 1980s and placed it on the right side of the mansion in a grassy area most guests weren't allowed to go, which was near the disability access entrance. She had Chris Goosman write funny epitaphs for the animals. An urban legend told about the hidden pet cemetery, and it became a hit with cast members at every level. In 1993, a pet cemetery moved into the attractions queue, but rumor has it the original cemetery still exists.

Just as the pet cemetery and the hearse added to the Haunted Mansion, Gracey and Crump were using older magic tricks and making them better. "The illusions Yale and I were perfecting were based on the 'black art boxes' and 'spirit cabinets' that had been used for many years by magicians," said Crump. "We did a lot of stuff like that, always trying to carry the illusion a step further" (Surrell, 2015, p. 18).

These weren't the only additions. After the success of the "it's a small world" holiday overlay, the imagineers decided to cook up a new overlay. They chose the Haunted Mansion. After considering several different variations including "A Christmas Carol," they decided that Disney already had the perfect opportunity for a new overlay in "The Nightmare

Before Christmas." In 2001, Jack Skellington took over the Haunted Mansion from just before Halloween through the New Year creating a wonderful place where two holidays collide. It has remained a holiday classic attraction ever since with its rhyming ghost host and its ever-changing, real gingerbread house.

In 2015, the Hatbox Ghost returned to the Haunted Mansion after years of speculation about why he left. These big changes aren't something Disney had to do. The Haunted Mansion is a classic attraction that has its fans and didn't need to have more added to it. However, even the best attractions can be made better, more engaging and newer with a touch of creativity. Even something small, like adding a Hidden Mickey, can improve the experience for guests visiting the Haunted Mansion.

Songwriter Richard Sherman said that Walt Disney "always had a way of 'plussing' a good idea" (Kurtti, 2008, p. 109). You can do the same thing with your own processes and when finding solutions. Even if you have an answer that works, you may want to go on looking for more solutions. Oftentimes, the first solution isn't the best, even when it works.

Artist Jasper Schellekens suggests that people "explore more options than are given." Going further in the process will help you gather more solutions, and possibly improve in areas you didn't know needed improvement.

Imagineer Joe Parinella said that "even when a project is done, it's not finished. You can always go back and add more; you can always go one better" (Kurtti, 2008, p. 65).

Moving forward takes you to the mausoleum. The wall with the names of the dearly departed is below the queue and on the left. The first section features arches in rows of three. The top row houses the last resting place of "Theo Later," "U. R. Gone" and "Ray N. Carnation." In the second row rest the remains of "Dustin T. Dust," "Levi Tation" and "I.M. Mortal." At the lowest level, "G. I. Missyou" is the only resident. The next section of the mausoleum holds rectangular memorials for "I. Trudy Departed" and "Rustin Peece" in the top row. "I. L. Beback" and "M. T. Tomb" are in the middle row. The bottom has no inhabitants. The path below the queue leads to a cemented wall that looks like a crypt with no entrance and a closed metal door next to it.

As the queue snakes around, you might notice lights in the mansion. The line goes onto the wrap-around porch area and leads you to the front of the house. People are let in from the FASTPASS line and the regular line to total about 40 for each group. Everyone assembles in the entry hall and waits for directions. Eerie music plays, a cold breeze disturbs the air.

The Butler and Maid – Find and Be a Mentor

A butler and maid, grim in demeanor, open the door to the mansion and usher you in. That uneasy feeling, reinforced by the pet cemetery, the mausoleum and the graves on the hill makes sense. After a day in the "happiest place on Earth," you realize the butler and maid aren't smiling. They are tight-lipped and emotionless. One or the other might even be frowning. Their loud, monotone voices as they issue instructions and count the number of people coming into the foyer undercut the murmurs of the crowd.

The butler is dressed in a jacket with tails. The jacket is green with black trim at the collar and purple buttons. The pants match the green color. His shoes are black. Under the jacket is a light purple vest, which is horizontally striped in dark purple and has gold buttons. It covers a white shirt, and he wears a black tie.

The maid wears an apron, fringed in white lace and tied at the waist, that matches her top. Both are green with thick vertical purple stripes. The shirt has black buttons and puffy sleeves that end in white lace. The collar also has white lace. The dress under the apron is green and thick. It flows toward the ground just above her black shoes. The maid's hair is tied back with white lace that is home to a black bat bow. The butler and maid are there to help people find their way into the Haunted Mansion while avoiding the dangers that come with crowds. Mentors can help you find your creative path personally or in an organization.

Yale Gracey was a tinkerer, and Rolly Crump said he was Gracey's apprentice of a sort.

"Yale was the leading force," said Crump. "I was really just helping him, building boxes. I was actually learning from Gracey" (Baham, p. 33). Crump's modesty is belied by the fact that he came up with some original ideas that stumped Walt Disney until Disney came up with the idea for the Museum of the Weird, a now-never-materialized idea for a spill area with its own entrance and exit where guests could linger.

Kurtti (2008) said that Walt Disney nurtured Blaine Gibson's sculpting hobby into a career (p. 74). "He made it possible for me to have a career that was absolutely something I wouldn't have dreamed of as a farm boy" (Kurtti, 2008, p. 77). Gibson was responsible for sculpting Abraham Lincoln for "Great Moments with Mr. Lincoln." He did many of the pirates for "The Pirates of the Caribbean," and he did many of the ghosts for the Haunted Mansion. As an animator, Gibson as mentored by Frank Thomas.

Writer Chris Demetriou at Copper Mouflon advises those who want to be more creative to "be around creative people," and his advice is backed by research. Zhou (in 2003 as cited by Choi, Anderson and Veillette, 2009) found that working with creative coworkers can enhance an individual's creativity because the coworkers provided role modeling for creative techniques and problem-solving skills.

According to author Frank Barron (Barron, Montuori and Barron, 1997), creativity is "something that can be nurtured in others close to us" (p. 5). Teachers and parents can nurture creativity in the children they care for. More importantly, creativity skills get transferred both from the mentor to the one being mentored and vice versa.

However, in order to do so, people have to be aware of their own biases and actions. Decision makers and authority figures often say they value creativity, "but when tested, they do not value creators" (Ashton, 2015, p. 84). Teachers have the same problem because those who are more creative are harder to control. In a classroom with 30 children or an organization with thousands of employees, it's easier to be in charge if everyone is doing what is expected. It's much more difficult to govern and lead when people are being "playful, unconventional, and unpredictable."

Barron (Barron, Montuori and Barron, 1997) points out that your creative mentors don't have to be living. You can be inspired and mentored by the creative works of others, including books, films, inventions and novel enterprises (p. 6), like, perhaps, the Haunted Mansion and its team of creators.

The Foyer – Practice

The chandelier above is covered in cobwebs, and the candles flicker. The parquet wood flooring looks like its own spiderweb. On the same wall as the entrance is a window covered in lacy curtains with a mirror set perpendicular to it that catches the light and reflects. The wood panes are light and heavy with a like-colored valance at the top of the window frame. A sconce between the entrance and the window and another between the mirror and first set of doors hold candles. Across from the entrance are two light wood, double doors sitting perpendicular to each other; one is directly across from the entrance. There is a sconce between them. Next to the double doors opposite the entrance is another sconce of candles. A single door is in the third wall next to a mirror and a window that, regardless of what seems to be outside, is always dark. A final sconce is between this window and the entrance. According to DoomBuggies.com, the wallpaper is "Lily -- Dresser edition II." In the low illumination of the candlelight, it's hard to tell if the colors are gold, green and pink.

The entrance closes. In spite of all the candles and the chandelier, the room is poorly illuminated. A voice intones:

"When hinges creak in doorless chambers, and strange and frightening sounds echo through the halls. Whenever candle lights flicker where the air is deathly still, that is the time when ghosts are present, practicing their terror with ghoulish delight!"

Just like the ghosts practice their terror, you need to practice your creativity. Because creativity is a skill, some people will have more talent, and others will have to work harder at it. With practice, you can become more creative.

The Beatles burst on the scene in 1962 with "Love Me Do" and followed that with four more chart-topping hits within the year. Paul McCartney and John Lennon met in 1957. George Harrison came on board in 1958. Ringo Starr was a latecomer who joined the group in 1962 but had performed with the band numerous times before. It was practice that landed them in the position to have a successful, creative outburst (Weisberg, p. 238). They maximized their talent through practice and playing together.

In a story about canoeing in "Everything All at Once," Bill Nye said that he knew what to do to avoid a rock that would've capsized his canoe, but the knowledge only came with "confidence bred by repetition" (p. 31). The years of practice before allowed him to see everything at once and come up with a solution to the problem.

"The more you create, the more you are able to create" (Fritz, p. 33).

"Draw something that you're terrible at every single day," says artist Travis Bundy (2018). The more you draw, the better you'll get at it. The same is true of any skill, including creativity.

"Write, do your creative process, do your art every single day," says author Carrie Merrill (2017). You'll get good at it.

"You have to draw every day. No exceptions, no excuses. Draw every day." Draw what you're not comfortable with. "That is true of all aspects of creativity. Write every day. No excuses, no compromise... Creativity is a muscle, and if you don't use it, it doesn't get stronger," says Blacky Shepherd (2017), passing along advice he got from the artists he admired and talked to before he got into comics.

Echoing Shepherd's idea of creativity, Daniel Scully (2017) says, "Creativity is more of a muscle than a gift... It's a muscle you have to work at."

"You have to make art every day whether you feel like it or not in order to get somewhere," says artist Lisa Solomon (Congdon, 2014, p. 24). Doing something every single day is important to developing good habits with your time. Even if all you do is something small that only takes 15 minutes, it's still important to make the time and effort.

The Haunted Mansion went through several practice runs before it opened. Ken Anderson set up practice runs in 1957; Rolly Crump and Yale Gracey used practice runs in 1959 (Surrell, 2015, p. 18-19). The practices allowed the imagineers to see how the show would perform before it was in place permanently. They noticed that certain scenes took too long and that guests would linger and not move on to the next scene if they missed something. These early runs were part of the reason the Haunted Mansion didn't debut on schedule. It took time, practice, and the development of technology to create the attraction as it is today.

"Practice is always more important than theory" (Fritz, p. 169). There's always going to be something new to learn and something more to know even if you are or become the top expert in your field. At some point, you need to move away from the books, the thoughts and the intentions, and you need to move to actually doing. If you want to be a painter, you need to paint. If you want to be a writer, you need to write. If you want to be an ice cream maker, you need to make ice cream. As long as you can keep your thinking flexible, you can start creating now. All you have to do is step into the next room where you'll stretch your imagination.

The Stretching Room – Stretch Your Imagination

One set of the double doors opens, and you step through into an octagonal room. A deep voice comes from no discernible point, "Welcome, foolish mortals, to the Haunted Mansion. I am your host... your ghost host. Kindly step all the way in please and make room for everyone. There's no turning back now... Our tour begins here in this gallery, where you see paintings of some of our guests as they appeared in their corruptible, mortal state."

There are four pictures on the wall and gargoyles holding candles in each hand stare down at you menacingly. The pictures, in contrast, are pleasant portraits: a young girl in pink with a parasol, a seated old woman holding a red rose, a distinguished looking gentleman with a beard, and another distinguished looking gentleman with mutton chops.

"For a better view of our portraits, kindly drag your bodies away from the walls and to the dead center of the room," the butler says. There is a sound of sliding, the butler disappears, and there's the banging of something closing. The floor lowers.

"Your cadaverous pallor betrays an aura of foreboding, almost as though you sense a disquieting metamorphosis. Is this haunted room actually stretching? Or is it your imagination, hmm?"

The pictures seem to be getting longer and revealing more to the portraits that hang on the wall. The young woman with the parasol stands on a tightrope in ballet shoes; below her is a hungry looking crocodile swimming in a river his mouth gapes open waiting for her to fall.

The old woman, Abigail Patecleaver, is seated on a headstone that reads 'Rest in Peace\ Dear Beloved George.' Below is a bust of a man with a large moustache and a hatchet buried in the top of his bald head.

The distinguished man with the beard, Alexander Nitrokoff, isn't wearing pants. He's wearing red-striped, white boxers, and standing on a barrel labeled 'Dynamite." A poorly placed candle has lit a fuse leading to the barrel.

The man with the mutton chops sits on the shoulders of another man with white hair and a white moustache; the man appears concerned with something below him. He, in turn, sits on the shoulders of a third man with a chin curtain beard, who is frightened to the point of panic. His hands clench tight together as he holds the legs of the second man. He is up to his waist in quick sand and staring at the sign that should have warned them of the danger.

"And consider this dismaying observation: this chamber has no windows and no doors... which offers you this chilling challenge: to find a way out!" the ghost host laughs. "Of course, there's always my way." The Ghost Host laughs maniacally.

Lightning flashes and thunder crashes. The lights go out. More lightning from above, the wood panel ceiling is gone. A body hangs from the rafters. The lights go out again. There's a scream and the sound of bones breaking as the body hits the floor.

The stretching room harnesses your imagination by turning out the lights. You hear the body drop and feel the thud of the bones. While the Ghost Host's solution to getting out of room was extreme, it is only one solution to the puzzle. Using your imagination, you may be able to come up with other ways.

Albert Einstein said, "Imagination is more important than knowledge" (Maisel, 1995, p. 29). Imagination is the basis of creativity. All to often people forget to nurture their imagination and improve it through practice and the addition of new tools. Your dreams are pure imagination. It's the combining facility of the human brain that takes the day's anxieties and events and turns them into something fantastic and sometimes awful. Keeping a dream journal is one way to harness your imagination.

However, to really strengthen your imagination, it takes active engagement in thinking. Passive entertainment like television will drain you of your energy, imagination and creativity unless you're watching something that you don't normally watch. Watching shows that are outside of your wheelhouse can help engage the imagination if you think about them after wards. It isn't just enough to consume; you must also engage with the entertainment.

Books are better for your imagination because they don't provide you with the picture of what's going on. Sculptor

Blaine Gibson, who did the ghosts for the Haunted Mansion, used books to help harness is ability to sculpt. He would read the description of the characters and create small models of them (Kurtti, 2008, p. 75). He had to use his imagination to interpret the look of the character. The same will be true for you, even if you don't sculpt, paint or draw them. Read books outside your comfort zone. If you normally read detective stories or romance, try fantasy or classics. Science fiction is also good for looking at possible futures.

Daydreaming is something that we don't give ourselves enough time for. In today's busy world, it's difficult to justify sitting on a chair or porch and gazing into space while looking inward. The more you daydream, the more you'll be able to exercise your imagination. Turn off the phone, eliminate other distractions like music and allow your mind to wander wherever it will go. If you have a problem with doing nothing, try meditation and yoga practices first.

Writing can help you harness your imagination and practice using it. Find stories to tell and write them down. Exercising your imagination is about making stuff up in this case. Even if you've had an ordinary day, you can tell an alternative story about it. Share the story with someone you trust.

Playing dress-up doesn't just have to happen during Halloween. Make an outfit and take it to a local comic convention or dress up with your child. Both the acts of creating the outfit and then pretending like you're the character will exercise your imagination.

Part of being able to combine elements is actually knowing about different areas of knowledge. Asking questions is one of the best ways to get new information. Don't rely on the Internet. Instead, find a way to learn and remember the answers to the questions so the information is in your mind when you need it.

Make no mistake, your imagination is powerful. If you've ever imagined a negative consequence to something you were doing or you've experienced psychosomatic illnesses, it's due to your imagination. Only you can harness it to create in a positive way for you and the world. It just takes a little practice and a dash of courage to imagine how things can be better and then to implement those ideas.

"Oh, I didn't mean to frighten you prematurely." The lights come on. "The real chills come later. Now, as they say, 'look alive,' and we'll continue our little tour. And let's all stay together, please."

The Portrait Gallery – Embrace Change

A wall opens, and people crowd out of the Stretching Room. You notice pictures on the righthand side of the wall. On the left, you can see the outside where it's perpetually dark and rainy. Red velvet ropes and stanchions, with brass bats carved on top of them, line the hall. Lightning flashes on your left and the pictures on your right change.

"There are several prominent ghosts who have retired here from creepy old crypts all over the world. Actually, we have 999 happy haunts here — but there's room for 1,000. Any volunteers?" The Ghost Host laughs. "If you insist on lagging behind, you may not need to volunteer."

A woman reclines on a couch and becomes a white tiger when the lightning flashes. A knight with his sword raised sits on a rearing horse. The lightning flashes, and they both become skeletons. A dapper man's portrait, rumored to be the master of the house, also becomes a skeleton. A ship sailing the sea becomes a wreck facing a storm, and a beautiful woman becomes a medusa.

Just as the pictures in the gallery change to become something scary, creativity creates change that others will find scary. "By its nature creativity challenges the status quo, questions the correctness of procedures, and generally upsets the usual order of things. The resulting change can disturb and even frighten people" (Ealy, 1995, p. 203).

People are reticent to change because it's more difficult than not changing. Even for people who understand that change will always happen, rearranging habits, including habitual ways of thinking can be extremely difficult and induce stress. In spite of the plethora of quotes and folk wisdom that explain the nature of change as the only constant of life, people feel safer when everything remains the same. Even when it is clear that the proposed change is for the better, most people would rather deny its benefits than make the necessary changes.

One story to illustrate this reluctance to change involves the medical field and handwashing. As told by Ashton (2015, p. 72-74), Dr. Semmelweis in 1847 believed that doctors at Vienna General were the cause of women and babies dying. They would go from examining corpses to delivering babies, and in the process, 18 percent of their patients would die. The clinic next door had no cadavers and the mortality rate was two percent. Women and babies had a better survival rate giving birth in the street rather than in the clinic with the doctors.

Semmelweis initiated handwashing in his clinic and the mortality rate immediately dropped. Yet, his medical peers across the globe derided Semmelweis and his assertion because they believed that a gentleman's hands were always clean and all doctors were gentlemen. They also said that his scientific process in the question of handwashing was less than adequate. Germ theory was still waiting for Louis Pasteur, and the criticism of Semmelweis was so intense that, within a couple of years, he had lost his practice, his sanity, and his life.

Doctors went back to not washing their hands, and women and children went back to dying in that clinic and elsewhere.

Semmelweis had the data to back up the change, but because it threatened the identity of the people involved (doctors), it was rejected. Semmelweis thought they would just accept handwashing because it clearly saved lives, he couldn't understand why his fellow men of science would reject a practice that was obviously beneficial to the patients. He didn't realize that change is scary and represents a threat.

When someone proposes something new to you, how do you react? If you find yourself rejecting new suggestions out of hand, it may be because of the change it represents. Instead of fearing change, you should realize that change will happen whether we want it to or not. If you know that change is coming, you can prepare yourself for it, adapt to it, and sometimes, direct it. And if you're unsure, change is coming. Don't let it hit you like a lightning bolt from a storm. Seek it out, embrace it, and lead others to it.

The gallery is lined with gold chains connected to brass-colored bat stanchions to keep guests from getting to close to the windows and portraits. The bats extend their wings to maintain hold on the stanchions. The windows have open drapes in red velvet and gold fringe. The walls are lined with black wood paneling on the bottom half and a rich gold wallpaper above it. Chandeliers above and lights on the walls dimly light the corridor.

The Busts – Change Your Perspective

At the end a pair of busts, one resembling Caesar and the other looking like a schoolmarm, watch every move you make from their resting places in arched alcoves. Their eyes and face turn toward you no matter where you go.

When Yale Gracey and Rolly Crump were working on a different effect using an Abraham Lincoln mask as a base, Crump realized that when he stood behind the mask and saw its inverted form, the eyes seemed to follow him wherever he went (Gennawey, 2014, p. 248). The effect was disconcerting and worked no matter where the viewer was in the room.

It was the view from a different point that allowed the discovery of this effect. In the same way, changing your perspective can help you find new solutions and become more creative.

You may change your perspective literally. Stand on your head or look at the problem from underneath or above. Disney's "Big Hero 6" features Hiro's brother picking him up, turning him upside down and shaking him to get Hiro to change his perspective when solving a problem. Simply taking a step back and looking at the problem from farther away can improve your creative solutions.

You may also change your perspective figuratively. Taking on a different role, profession or point of view can help you imagine how you might solve the problem if you were someone else. You could look at it from a medical perspective, a military perspective, or a taxi driver's perspective. You could even take on the persona of your favorite creative person and ask what he or she would do. Try thinking about how an animal would approach the problem or become an inanimate object and see it from that point of view.

If you have problems with changing your own perspective, you might ask for help from someone who is different from you. However, instead of asking about the specific problem, start the conversation by asking about the person's problem-solving strategies in general.

To make use of this technique, you may need to do some research. Asking people questions about their lives, watching documentaries and reading books are great ways to get different perspectives. Reading fiction has been found to help people improve their empathy, which will help you see things from a different point of view.

As the old joke goes: How many imagineers does it take to change a light bulb? Does it have to be a light bulb? Maybe the perspective you need to change is at the level of the question.

The corridor narrows as you turn the corner and continue into the next room.

A Limbo of Boundless Mist – Tolerate Ambiguity

"And now, a carriage approaches to take you into the boundless realm of the supernatural. Take your loved ones by the hand, please, and kindly watch your step. Oh yes, and no flash pictures, please. We spirits are frightfully sensitive to bright lights." On the wall to your left cobwebs and candelabras sit inside while just beyond is "a limbo of boundless mist and decay" (*The Story and Song from the Haunted Mansion* (1969) as cited in Surrell, 2015, p. 85).

Any time you make something new, there'll be some ambiguity like a mist that clouds your opportunity to see or understand the outcome.

Fortunately, even the imagineers involved with the Haunted Mansion faced the same problem. "We didn't know what we were doing," said Rolly Crump (Baham, p. 33). "We were just playing around and didn't know how we were going to use it" (Kurtti, 2008, p. 67).

"Uncertainty (or ambiguity) is an aversive state: we avoid it if we can" (Ashton, p.86). "For many people the unknown creates a sense of conflict, disorientation, and discomfort" (Fritz, p. 58.) People want to know what's going to happen next. They want predictability. "Although the unknown is not really a threat, many people treat it as such" (Fritz, p. 58).

One story says that when Disney's Animal Kingdom was first built, it didn't have any directional signs in the plaza after the entrance. There were a series of paths with no designation;

the imagineers thought it would lend itself to the atmosphere of adventure. People would take a path just to see where it would lead. The imagineers were wrong. The lack of directions created a bottleneck as people came to a stop and tried to find the right path. In a place that was supposed to encourage exploration, that was built for fun, people did not want to choose the wrong path. Disney's Animal Kingdom installed path markers, and the bottleneck cleared up.

"Starting is scary. It brings up fears for all of us, beginners and advanced artists alike, because we are stepping into the unknown" (Bloomston, p. 10). Staring at the blank page or the blank canvas is often the hardest part for any creative because there's no way to know what the outcome will be. Just making a mark can be an opening enough for a bock to be broken. Even when you're not sure where you're going, as Walt Disney said, "The way to get started is to quit talking and begin doing" (BrainyQuotes, 2019).

"Tolerance of ambiguity is considered a valuable trait for creativity because there is often a phase in which incompatible, ill-defined elements coexist during problem solving" according to Lubart (p. 344). Creation and creativity aren't predictable. You may not know the outcome of the experiments you're conducting, but you shouldn't be fearful of trying something new. By tolerating ambiguity, you can take a new path that may not end up where you think it does. Stare into the boundless mist of limbo and be curious about it. Ask yourself what it is you want to see and what you need to see, then sit with your lack of knowledge and allow the ambiguity to direct you.

The Doom Buggies – Keep the Ideas Flowing

People are already in the Doom Buggies headed up a stairwell.

According to an interview in "The 'E' Ticket" with Ken Anderson, Walt said "We're going to use all the ideas we've ever had, and we're going to invent more… we'll need all kinds of ideas and ways of doing things that we haven't thought of yet. But they will be thought of" (as cited in Baham, 2014, p. 14)

The Haunted Mansion concept started as a walk-through. Groups of people were tested walking through the sets of Zorro. A mock-up was made on a sound stage in December 1957, and people were led through just as if the attraction were at Disneyland. The goal was to be able to move 40 people through each room in 90 seconds. That goal was unattainable as a walking tour. A week later Ken Anderson suggested a vehicle, but the technology for the vehicle wasn't available, yet.

With the success of the Pirates of the Caribbean, there was some talk about having the mansion sinking into a Louisiana bayou and using boats for the tour. Yale Gracey worked on a model for this idea, but the concept was discarded because there were already a number of boat attractions at Disneyland.

Disneyland Operations Director Dick Nunis wanted an attraction that would serve as many people as possible in an hour. His insistence on greater ride capacity earned him the nickname "Hopalong Capacity" (Surrell, 2015, p. 30). With the invention of the Omnimover system used at Adventure thru Inner Space, the Haunted Mansion found a way to move over 2,500 people through the attraction in an hour.

"The Omnimover, it's the ride system that never stops," said imagineer Bruce Gordon (Aitken, 2007A).

The constant flow of people through the Haunted Mansion is just what you want for ideas through your organization, especially at the beginning of a creative endeavor. Rolly Crump had submitted well over a hundred ideas for the Haunted Mansion starting from the time when he began working on the show in the late 1950s (Surrell, 2015, p. 27).

"We spent a year coming up with as many ideas, as much imagination, as we could," said Crump (1993 "Disney News" article as cited in Surrell, 2015, p. 19). Crump's ideas didn't just stop at the brainstorming stage; in 1964, Rolly Crump set about developing some of them for his new, Walt-christened "Museum of the Weird" (Surrell, 2015, p. 27).

Linus Pauling said the secret to success was to "think a lot of ideas and throw away the bad ones" (as cited in Csikszentmihalyi, 1999, p. 332). Artist Roger Langridge agreed saying, "The more ideas you throw at the wall, the more good ones you're going to have."

Brainstorming is a popular technique that works well for generating ideas. Walt Disney spent time brainstorming ideas with his staff according to Steven Watts (as cited in Kurtti,

2008, p. vii). The Disney imagineers call this blue sky thinking, and according to "The Imagineering Field Guide to Disneyland," they follow four rules:

>   1. There is no such thing as a bad idea…
>   2. We don't talk yet about why not…
>   3. Nothing should stifle the flow of ideas…
>   4. There is no such thing as a bad idea… (We take that one seriously.) (p. 12)

These rules are designed to help people come up with more ideas while brainstorming allows people to build off one another. "The sparks come from ideas rubbing against each other rather than as bolts out of the blue" (Isaacson, p. 110).

Brainstorming was developed by Alex Osborn and advertising executive in 1939. Not everyone thinks that it works. Author Kevin Ashton (p. 50) cites a study using scientists and ad executives from 3M. Brainstorming in groups of 4 produced fewer ideas and less quality in those ideas than individuals alone during the same time span. In separate studies that used larger groups, the ideas and their quality further degraded.

Ashton also looked at studies that showed deferred judgement just resulted in more bad ideas within groups. If ideas were judged as the session went along, the group produced fewer ideas overall, but they produced the same number of good ideas as the group that didn't judge.

Ashton isn't the only one to call brainstorming into question as a way to develop ideas. Edward de Bono (2015) also thinks brainstorming is wasteful. De Bono sees far too many sessions where people try to come up with the most outlandish idea. Robert Fritz finds brainstorming "a rather inefficient, ineffective, and indirect step" (p. 25).

The biggest problem with brainstorming is that many companies fail to record, keep and follow up on the ideas that are brought up in during the sessions. Having an idea isn't enough to be creative, you must follow through on the idea and complete the project.

The bats and chains mark the pathway to follow. Chandeliers hanging above are covered in cobwebs, too. The right side is not any cleaner as cobwebs form arched designs from the walls to the candelabras. On the floor are large pots, urns if you will, from which black light emanates. The path continues to narrow until it only permits one person into the left turn that runs by a bannister. This leads to a turnstile.

The vertical parts of a turnstile ensure that only one person gets onto the moving walkway. An usher calls out, "Two or three bodies per buggy, please," and points to the carriage you are supposed to take.

Sitting in the Doom Buggy, the ghost host returns behind you and just over your shoulder. "Do not pull down on the safety bar, please. I will lower it for you. And heed this warning: the spirits will materialize only if you remain safely seated with your hands, arms, feet, and legs inside. And watch your children, please." The safety bar floats down to enclose the buggy, and reaches the foot of the stairs.

The Endless Hallway – Be Curious

On either side of the stairway is a griffin, its claws extended outward. A candelabra on a pedestal towers over each of them. The buggy climbs the stairwell in the dark. At the top of the stairs, the Doom Buggy turns to the right. The Ghost Host says, "We find it delightfully unlivable here in this ghostly retreat. Every room has wall-to-wall creeps, and hot and cold running chills. Shhh, listen!"

Around the corner a candle on a tall pole provides illumination. Gray plants sit on the floor, and a suit of armor moves its shield up and down and its pole arm back and forth. The shield is a rounded triangular shape divided into four sections. The upper left has a red cross with a yellow background. The upper right has a stylized prancing lion on a gray background. The lower parts have 'x' shapes in gray and red. The helmet is shaped like a bird's head with a bent beak. Gold eyebrows are bent fiercely over golden eyes. Plumes of yellow and red flow from the top. The knight's shoulder guards are decorated with the fleur-de-lys. Red velvet hangs from the bottom of his chest plate.

The Doom Buggy rolls in front of a corridor that goes on forever. Candelabras and cobwebs hang from the ceiling of the corridor. A set of steps leads up to the carpeted hallway and wood doors line it. At some point in the distance a candelabra floats in a circle above the floor. What's at the end of the endless hallway? How does that candelabra float there? It's good to be curious.

"We keep moving forward -- opening up new doors and doing new things -- because we're curious, and curiosity keeps leading us down new paths. We're always exploring and experimenting. We call it Imagineering, the blending of creative imagination and technical know-how," said Walt Disney (Surrell, 2015, p. 11).

Curiosity is the way to learning. Children are naturally curious. They ask why. They explore the borders. They keep asking questions until adults get irritated, and the children ask more. They want to know about the world and why things are the way they are. Unfortunately, this curiosity is often punished rather than rewarded.

Adult life gets to be too busy for curiosity. People don't have time to explore. They don't have time to wonder. They settle for things the way they've always been done. They go to places they always go. This leads to a dull and uninteresting life. It also stifles creativity.

According to Csikszentmihalyi, "the most salient characteristic of creative individuals is constant curiosity" (1999, p. 330).

Filmmaker Federico Fellini (Barron, Montuori, and Barron, 1997, p. 34) said that "as a man, I am interested in everything, and as far as what you call problems are concerned, I go in search of them because I am curious and anxious to learn."

Psychologist Donald Campbell believes that "the difference between a scholar who comes up with new ideas and one who does not is often a difference of curiosity" (Csikszentmihalyi, 2013, p. 86).

"When we act on our curiosity, we feed our brains and are in the greatest position to enrich our lives" says author Todd Kashdan (p. 17).

Bob Gurr said that when Walt Disney "would get curious about something, he'd go at it quite thoroughly" (Kurtti, 2008, p. 102). Gurr said that he wasn't sure how Walt could do so with his busy schedule, but thought that walking around might have something to do with it. "Walt was totally informed by informing himself – if he was curious, he would ask a guy about something. That's a very crucial thing."

Just like the Endless Corridor, your curiosity should have no end. Keep asking questions, keep exploring, and keep being more creative. On the other side of the entrance to the corridor is a red velvet chair with white fringe and a face on its back. While some say it bears a resemblance to the designs of Rolly Crump and his use of human forms as architecture and design, others believe it's a hidden Donald Duck. A pole with a candle on top signals the end of the room.

The Conservatory – Believe You Can

The Doom Buggy backs into the conservatory. Pictures of ghost residents line the wall on the left. On the right is a raven with glowing red eyes atop a wreath covered in cobwebs. Decaying plants are in death bloom throughout the area, and a coffin sits in the center with a not-quite-dead occupant. His hands push up the lid to the coffin, and he reveals his skeletal arms. "Let me out, let me out of here!" He implores while pushing the coffin lid up. It's too heavy for him, and on top of the lid are two candlesticks undisturbed by the coffin occupant's movements. Another wreath is at the coffin's head.

The key to freeing your inner creativity isn't reliant on anyone other than you. The first thing that you need is the belief not only that you are creative, but that you can also become more creative. This is a case where Henry Ford's assertion that "whether you think you can or you can't, you're right," is true and backed by scientific research. People who believe they can become more creative and work at it, do become more creative.

"All of us are genetically pre-wired for innovation" according to Dr. David Pensak (McDonald, p. 190). There are many reasons why you may doubt your creativity, but if you want to boost your belief that you're creative, you only have to look in three places: your childhood, your dreams and your fears.

As a child, you probably played games, you may have had an imaginary friend, and you may have enjoyed reading books. You might have colored in books, on paper or on the wall. You might have even had your drawings displayed on the refrigerator. You probably told people what you wanted to be when you grew up, and your ideas about a good career probably changed with time. Maybe you imagined what you would get from the ice cream man, but you didn't have any money. Perhaps, you lied once or twice to your parents, teachers or other authority figures. These are all examples of being creative. While lying is generally immoral, it still takes creativity to think about something that is different from reality. In fact, all of these activities require the imagination and creativity.

Maybe you don't remember your dreams, but you have them. If you do recall your dreams, they probably aren't always realistic. You're at work, but it's really the grocery store. You're flying. You're fighting dinosaurs with a Cuisinart. Even your mundane dreams probably aren't realistic. If you don't remember your dreams, go to bed and tell yourself you will. When you get up write down what you remember immediately.

Whatever you fear, your imagination has blown out of proportion. If you think about doing taxes wrong and the taxman coming to take your belongings, that takes imagination. If you think about all of the terrible things that can happen when your child is out of your sight, that takes imagination. If you're afraid of climate change, birds attacking, or giant hamster zombies, that takes imagination. If you have anxiety that you can describe and put a name to, you have imagination, and imagination is the basis of all creativity.

    The corpse in the coffin needs help to be freed, but you can free your creativity through your belief in yourself.

The Corridor of Doors – Have Courage

The Doom Buggy continues its backwards tour through the corridor of doors. The portraits on the walls are more visible here, and they feature some of the residents of the Haunted Mansion in their moldering states. Skeletal heads with hair sticking out in every direction and sardonic grins make these photos frightening. One portrait has a top hat-wearing ghost. Another features a ghost with long, white, stringy hair. Some of the pictures look like they repeat themselves, and quite a few are around a framed embroidery proclaiming "Tomb Sweet Tomb."

The wallpaper behind them adds a disquieting effect. The Mansion may be watching you. It's purple and black and contains eyes, faces and teeth everywhere.

The doors in this corridor are not quiet. Door knockers pound up and down. Door handles, which look like serpents with pointy tails and open mouths, move up and down loudly. One door looks like it's breathing. They have a lion's head carved into the center of them. There are clear sounds of spirits who are knocking from behind the doors.

To get through this corridor, it takes courage. In the same way, it takes courage to follow through on creative ideas. Having the idea isn't enough. You must do the work to bring that idea to life, and depending on what it is, that may mean facing ridicule and jeering from the sidelines.

"Never be afraid to do something new, something different and to challenge the idea, the notion of how things are normally done," said artist Jon Boy Meyers (2017).

Both Disneyland and "Snow White and the Seven Dwarfs" were referred to as "Walt's Folly." Walt Disney had the courage to put everything he owned on the line and to bring both ideas to their successful and world-changing conclusion. It took courage for Disney to put his reputation on the line and take a loan on his life insurance policy to start funding Disneyland. He even had to face criticism from his wife who wondered why he wanted to open a dirty amusement park and his brother who thought it was better to stick with movies.

"Don't be afraid to plunge head first into anything," said writer Michael Tanner (2018) of "Junior Braves of the Apocalypse."

In an interview with Alison Beard (2013), poet Maya Angelou said that courage is learned: "You develop courage by doing courageous things, small things, but things that cost you some exertion." So, whatever fears are holding you back, you can gain the courage by overcoming them a little at a time.

Being creative involves taking a part of yourself that you normally keep hidden and exposing it to the world. There's ego and emotions involved. Anytime, you take the risk to show others who you are, it's scary, and it takes courage. Whatever your idea is, it probably won't be accepted immediately. That's okay. It's just important for you to get your ideas out there and seen. It takes courage to show your work to the world. It takes greater courage to follow through on your dreams.

"Creativity takes courage," said Henri Matisse. Cultivate your courage one step at a time and be creative.

The Clock – Make Time

The grandfather clock in the next alcove strikes 13. One hand spins quickly around the face of the clock, which is surrounded by the teeth of a demon whose eyes are nested in the top of the clock's wood casing. It looks like the demon is swallowing time. The pendulum is a pointed demon's tail. With each swing the clock clicks off the seconds. Tick Tock, Tick Tock, Tick Tock... A shadow of a giant claw flashes over the clock.

In 1959, Rolly Crump and Yale Gracey were given time and space to develop ideas. "During that year, Yale and I developed many of the first versions of the illusions for the Haunted Mansion... Walt just wanted us to be left alone, and he gave us the freedom to do whatever we wanted" (Gennawey, p. 166).

Gracey wasn't given any deadlines. Instead, he just explored whatever interested him. Walt was happy with Gracey inventing things when they happened not on a deadline.

"Creative pursuits are time consuming. If one wants to write poetry or compose music, one must find time – lots of time – to write or compose" (Nickerson, p. 417). Oftentimes, getting into a creative endeavor takes warm up time. It's hard to just sit down and create. Instead, your mind has to be moved toward the act with intention. If it takes you 20 minutes to get warmed up, it's important for you to be able to spend additional time being creative. Too little time spent at doing the project will result in something that lacks the creativity you're capable of. For brainstorming sessions in a group or by yourself, the easy ideas come in the first 20 minutes, the most creative ideas come after the obvious ideas are exhausted.

Not everyone has the luxury that Gracey had in working with Walt and WED, aka Walt Disney Imagineering. Many people have deadlines for their work, financial pressures and jobs that aren't conducive to creativity. Still, carving out time for your own creativity is vital. KM Alexander (2017) believes that "time is the precious commodity that every creative works in."

You can't save time; you can't spend time. Time continues to march inexorably on no matter what you do. If you want to be creative, you have to harness the time and not get distracted by other pressures or responsibilities.

Setting aside the time to be creative may be the most difficult part of creativity for most people. Part of the problem is that many people don't prioritize creativity in their lives. It's hard to justify thinking because it doesn't look like your doing anything, and there appears to be no end product. Thinking is a large part of creativity, and you need to set aside time for it as much as you need time to actually do your creative activity.

It's also difficult to say "no" to requests from others. If someone asks for a favor, it's natural to want to agree to it because you don't want to be seen as aloof or as a snob. However, when these requests take the place of doing something creative, they can be destructive.

As Charles Dickens pointed out (Ashton, p. 71-72), the invitation to coffee may only take 15 minutes from the person doing the invitation, but it could take the entire day from the creative person. Starting with the need to choose an appropriate outfit, getting to the venue, ordering and socializing, and returning to the place of creativity, will be more than 15 minutes. If anything happens to disrupt the creative person's mood on the way including worrying about what he or she said during the conversation, a whole day could be lost. That time can never be gotten back.

You have to make the decision for yourself and know your own rhythms. Sometimes, the interview or social activity can help jump start your creativity. However, if you get invited to do something during the time when you're usually writing, painting, or thinking though the creative process, you might be better off suggesting a different time or saying no completely. Coming up with a set of criteria for accepting an invitation may help you in advance to be better able to say "no" and feel okay with it.

"Time is the raw material of creation" (Ashton, p. 70). Every person has a time during the day that he or she is most creative and most productive. While much of creativity is time in the chair or at the easel or with whatever instruments you use in your creative endeavors and time spent thinking, harnessing your natural rhythms can help jump start your creativity. When life gets in the way, though, you might have to adjust your internal rhythms. Create when the children are asleep. Create when you come home from work. Set aside some time every day to use your creativity; put it in your calendar. Guard that time jealously.

The Séance Circle – Synergy

On the back of the chair in the next room is a raven. Is it another raven, or the same one from the conservatory? A woman's voice is chanting. She's trying to summon the spirits. As the buggy comes around the chair, you see a table with a crystal ball floating above it. Inside the crystal ball is the woman's head, whose voice rings out with commands for the inhabitants the other world.

> "Serpents and spiders, tail of a rat, call in the spirits, wherever they're at! [Sounds of ghosts.] Rap on a table — it's time to respond. Send us a message from somewhere beyond… [Knock on table.] Goblins and ghoulies from last Halloween, awaken the spirits with your tambourine! [Sound of a tambourine.] Creepies and crawlies, toads in a pond, let there be music from regions beyond! [A brass instrument plays part of 'Grim Grinning Ghosts.'] Wizards and witches, wherever you dwell, give us a hint, by ringing a bell! [A bell rings.] (Disney Park Scripts, 2017.)"

The table holds several candles and in front of it is a book on a pedestal. The book is opened with a picture of death on one side and "A Spell to Bring to Your Eyes and Ears One Who Is Bound in Limbo." The verses written below the title are the same as Madame Leota is chanting.

The instruments for the spirits responses are floating around the room. A light display represents the ghostly manifesting of energy. A floating table is where the rapping comes from. A drum, harp, long horn and cymbals float in a group for music from beyond. Another table floats while a lamp floats high above it. A trumpet floats around in a circle with a second horn and a tambourine.

It takes poetry, music, and magic to conjure the spirits. A book and tarot cards help. Each of these items has an energy of its own, but combined they bring the spirits to life. This type of synergy can also help you energize your own creative efforts. By participating in arts and subjects that aren't a part of your daily routine, you can harness techniques and thoughts to become more creative.

If you own a business, you can take lessons in synergy from the Walt Disney Company. They harness their intellectual property and use it in ways that help create a more robust bottom line. The Haunted Mansion itself has sparked a movie (admittedly bad) and tie-ins that include a Game of Life by Hasbro, a series of novels based on the 999 Happy Haunts, and a comic book series. There are figures at every price level, clothes, mouse ears, pins, and hundreds of other products available. At the exit, guest come across a gypsy cart selling some of the above-mentioned souvenirs. Disneyland harnesses the crowd going into the Haunted Mansion with a well-placed set of carts for snacks, including churros and popcorn that often comes in a haunted mansion themed souvenir bucket.

Your synergistic opportunities might not be so great, but if you look hard enough, you might find a way to get more out of the energy you spend than the average creative. For example, research for a novel can also be used to write blog posts which tie to the novel. If you have friends who are working on their creativity, you may be able to join forces to encourage each other and create something that neither of you would've thought of on your own.

The Grand Hall – A Stimulating Environment

"The happy haunts have received your sympathetic vibrations and are beginning to materialize. They're assembling for a swinging wake, and they'll be expecting me... I'll see you all a little later."

The Doom Buggies glide around a corner and the Grand Hall opens up below. The upper level of the hall has windows and torn curtains. Lightning flashes in the dark sky outside, and spirits fly in through the windows. Their arms outstretched; these apparitions don't seem to have any legs. Their clothes hang down from their bodies in like tattered fringe. On the right is a fireplace where, on the mantle a ghost sits hugging a bust. The ghost is wearing a stovepipe hat. Next to the bust is a long dead plant in an urn and other urns.

The fireplace glows green and a ghostly grandma rocks back and forth in a rocking chair while knitting. A hurricane lamp sits on a coffee table next to grandma. There is also a book and a tea set including a pot, sugar cup and milk cup. There is no tea cup to be seen. Grandma is dressed in a shawl and wears her glasses. (Rumor says she's the grandma from the Carousel of Progress.)

A hearse has backed through the wide-open double doors under the windows, and guests are arriving for this swinging wake. A coffin has spilled out of the hearse and onto the floor. Its lid is has slid partially off. A woman with a parasol, a boy with a rose, a sea captain who may be a pirate, a fat ghost with a top hat and cane and a woman in a bonnet with a picnic basket are among those who come in from the hearse.

A stairway leads to the library. At the bottom, a massive candelabra forms part of the bannister. The bannister itself is broken about halfway up the stairs. A red-eyed crow is on the upper level of the rail cawing at the guests from above.

A pair of dueling ghost portraits whose subjects come to unlife to turn and fire one-shot pistols at each other. Both wear top hats. The portraits are framed so they have their backs turned to each other. One has friendly mutton chops and a goatee; his face is set in grim determination. The other wears a sharply lined balbo. His beard coming to a point.

In the middle of the Grand Hall is a birthday party. The table is decked out in fine china and cobwebs. One of the settings is placed as a hidden Mickey. The birthday ghost with her hair in a bun blows out her thirteen candles. She leans over the table; her cheeks puffed out. When the candles go out, the ghosts disappear. But these appear to be trick candles; when they come on again, the party goers at the table reappear. A man with an old dutch beard sits to the right of the birthday girl. He holds a drink in his hand.

A man with a crown sits between him and another man who is pulling himself out from under the table. The king is old, has a goatee and a chain around his neck. The man pulling himself up to the table is wearing a night cap.

Great Caesar's Ghost is at the opposite end of the table as the birthday girl. He is wearing a laurel wreath and traditional roman robes. One guest has already had too much fun and has passed out under the table with only his legs to be seen. His chair is overturned and lies on its side. A bottle is next to the chair.

Pickwick the ghost hangs from the chandelier above the table. He is dressed in a top hat and a coat with tails. A scarf hangs down from his neck. His Dickensian look is how he got his name. His cane anchors him to the top of the chandelier as does his right foot. His left foot dangles out over the Grand Hall kicking back and forth. Two other ghosts, who might be Cleopatra and Mark Anthony, sit in the chandelier with Pickwick rocking from side to side. She has her arm entwined with his. All three ghosts hold glasses with a red drink in them; Pickwick holds his out as if toasting you, the passenger, in the Doom Buggy. The other two ghosts wave their glasses back and forth in time to the music.

Underneath the walkway to the library is a small end table with a potted plant. Next to it is a red velvet chair and another table with a chair on its other side. There is a lantern on the table.

The women lead the men as they dance to a waltz version of "Grim, Grinning Ghosts" played by the organist on the opposite wall across from the fireplace. They pass through the two chairs and coffee table that are placed on their dance floor. The women wear ball gowns and the men wear fancy suits typical of the late 1800s. Behind them is a couch with end tables on either side. As you pass by, you may notice a spider has taken up residence near one of the Grand Hall's columns.

Spirits arise from the organ with each note played. The organist wears a cape and top hat. There are two candelabras of five candles each on the organ. This is the same organ that was seen in Disney's "20,000 Leagues under the Sea."

There is so much going on in the Haunted Mansion's Grand Hall that guests have to ride through it several times to understand and see everything, and even that's not enough because the cast members and imagineers change the scene, most often through moving the Hidden Mickey on the table. This stimulating atmosphere was even more important when attractions were entered using a system of tickets. The more times a person rode an attraction, the more money that attraction made, and by extension, the more money Disneyland made. By making this scene, and the graveyard scene, so complex, Disneyland was able to give the Haunted Mansion a high revisit factor. People want to see what's going on in that scene.

Just like the activity in the Grand Ballroom, creativity requires a lively and complex environment that "provides varied opportunity for self-expression and personal involvement" and stimulates flexibility and spontaneity in those who are a part of it (Barron, Montuori, and Barron, 1997 p. 19), even when it is filled with the dead. Ray Bradbury provided his own stimulating environment in the form of his office where he would "never run out of ideas" (McLean and Lynch, 1989).

Pepper's Ghost – Making Something Old New Again

You may have noticed a spider web in the corridor as your Doom Buggy glides past the Grand Hall scene. The spider web hides a hole in the glass that was created when a guest shot the glass with a .22 caliber gun in the 1970s. Because of the size of the glass, the roof would have to be lifted off the Haunted Mansion to replace it. Instead, imagineers dressed it up and left it. The glass is an important part of allowing the ghosts to materialize while keeping people in their Doom Buggies safe.

Many guests are surprised to learn that the ghosts in the Grand Ballroom are not holograms. They are the result of a magic effect invented in Italy, propagated by Henry Dircks in the 1860s and improved upon and simplified by John Pepper. Now called "Pepper's Ghost," the illusion works on a principle of ray optics.

A sheet of clear glass is set up at a 45-degree angle to the audience. Behind the glass is the stage where all of the real props are. In a room to the front of the glass blocked from the view of the audience is a mirror image of the room behind the glass with the addition of the ghost(s). When the hidden room is lit up, the reflection off the glass looks like the ghost is in the room behind the glass. Turn out the lights illuminating the hidden room, and the ghost disappears. This effect has also been used in museums to create 3D effects and was used to create an onstage Tupac at a music festival.

Disneyland hosts one of the largest versions of Pepper's Ghost in the world, and it was Rolly Crump and Yale Gracey who enlarged the effect to achieve the spectacle in the ballroom. Gracey found the effect in a book called "The Boy Mechanic vol. 1" by Popular Mechanics (Baham, 2014, p. 35).

By repurposing Pepper's Ghost, Gracey was able to create convincing ghosts. The addition of audio-animatronics allows the effect to be performed over and over with no variation. Creativity isn't just about recombining or coming up with something new and useful; sometimes, it's about finding a new use for something that others have discarded or that they haven't considered. People often do this without thinking about it. A book isn't meant to prop open a door or prop up a table, but they can solve those problems adequately.

The Haunted Mansion is made new again in the latter part of the year when Jack Skellington and his Halloween-Christmas celebration takes over. This incarnation of the Haunted Mansion is different every year with the addition of new characters, like Sally who was added in the graveyard in 2016, and the changing of the real gingerbread house that gets more elaborate with each passing year. The idea itself came from the success of the it's a small world holiday overlay.

Giving an old idea new life is one way to make something old new again. Upcycling is another way. By taking something that you don't use anymore and turning it into something else, you get to exercise your creativity, and when the project works, you help save the planet. Too much of our waste ends up in the landfill or as pollution. Finding new ways to use old things will help make you feel better creatively and as a someone who is doing something good for the planet.

There is a table with a mirror above it and a pair of hats in the corridor the Doom Buggies are gliding through.

The Attic – Tell Your Story

The attic is darker than the Grand Hall. A trunk on your right is opened, and a ghost pops up for a jump fright. In front of it is a dish set. There is a table with a hurricane lamp, wedding album and lace. The marriage is dated as 1869. A framed photo on a chair just beyond the table shows a youthful man, Ambrose Harper, in a bowler hat and bow tie with his taller bride. He has a pocket kerchief. She wears one strand of pearls. The man's head disappears. There is a small clock and a couple of pieces of porcelain on a shelf. A carpet bag sits on the floor next to the chair. A ghostly giggle can be heard nearby, "I do and I did." There is a dollhouse behind the photo hidden in the shadows.

On the left side is another photo. The bride is the same. The man, Frank Banks, is taller, wearing a top hat and has a large moustache. The marriage is dated as 1872. She is wearing two strands of pearls. A banner proclaiming "True Love Forever, 1872, Frank and Constance" hangs above a large cache of porcelain. The man's head disappears. The voice says, "In sickness and in wealth."

On the right side, the picture is of a man of Asian descent, the Marquis. He's dressed in ceremonial clothes of the military with a sash and medals on his chest. He wears sideburns and a horseshoe moustache. The bride is the same, but she wears three strands of pearls now. The wedding photo is dated as 1874. An empty candelabra sits on the table with the photo, and an empty candlestick is on the floor next to the table. A bird cage covered in cobwebs hangs above the photo. The Marquis loses his head. "As long as we both shall live," says the ghostly voice.

The next photo features a seated man, Reginald, of large proportions. The same bride stands over him. The marriage is dated 1875. Reginald, in his top hat and holding a cane, is frowning at the camera. His mutton chop sideburns are substantial. The alcove has a tiger's skin and a globe as well as the cane that Reginald is holding in the photo. The bride wears the same wedding dress and four strands of pearls. He has ruby brooch on the right side of his vest. His head disappears. "For better or for worse," intones the bride.

A shadow plays "the Wedding March" on a piano, but it sounds like a funeral dirge. The piano is covered in cobwebs. "Here comes the bride," says the ghostly voice.

The bride stands in the alcove close to the attic window and next to a wedding cake. A photo of George is next to the cake. Is it the same George from the stretching room? With each phrase, the bride manifests a wry smile and an axe, presumably the weapon that has killed all of her husbands. "You may now kiss the bride," says Constance. "We'll live happily ever after."

Each alcove tells the story of the man Constance married and beheaded.

While many people claim that the Haunted Mansion, at least as it was originally built, had no story. It was a series of experiences. However, Jim Korkis (2014) has a different account of the Haunted Mansion's story. Korkis talked with imagineer Ken Anderson, who was the first imagineer assigned to the development of the attraction, several times before Anderson's death in 1993. Anderson asserted that the Haunted Mansion had a story. There was pirate who hid his identity in a trunk in the attic. He married a young woman and told her not to go into the attic. She did, and he caught her. Fearing she would reveal his secret, he threw her out the window of the attic to her death. She haunted him until he hanged himself in the stretching room. That's the story guests used to live out in the Haunted Mansion, and the elements are still there

Korkis said that Anderson was convinced that storytelling is what separated Disney attractions from carnival rides, so it is important that the Haunted Mansion have its own story. Anderson also believed that storytelling would help move the crowd from one room to the next, which was important because he was considering a walk-through attraction at that point in Haunted Mansion history.

Stories are more important to communities in a capacity greater than a theme park attraction and its flow through. Author Madeleine L'Engle says that stories bind people and societies together (Csikszentmihalyi, 2013, p. 257). Telling stories is essential for humanity. Stories are the way people pass their history from one generation to the next. From oral traditions and carvings to hieroglyphics and books to movies and television, stories infuse our world. Storytelling doesn't take place only in writing. Sculptures, dances, and paintings can tell stories. Disneyland and the Haunted Mansion are full of stories. We become the stories that are told about us as a society and as individuals.

When Marc Davis was brought out to Disneyland to look at the Mine Train through Nature's Wonderland, he noted the attraction lacked a story. The animals were on display without any narrative to help people understand what was going on. Davis restaged the animals and made the attraction better (Kurtti, 2008, p. 50).

As stated earlier, Walt didn't say he was building a ride with ghostly effects in an interview with the BBC. Instead, he said he was in Europe to collect ghosts, who were being displaced by modernization. They needed a place where they could perform, and Disneyland was going to provide them a place. This story led to Marty Sklar's sign out front of the Haunted Mansion and later to the attraction's overall storyline. It was Walt's seemingly-off-the-cuff story that was the impetus for the rest of the attraction. Even if the Haunted Mansion appears to be without a story, it has inspired several stories, including a 1969 album featuring Ron Howard and Robie Lester, and a series of more recent tales published in novel format.

Telling your story is important because no one has a story just like yours. Everyone has different perceptions, different memories and different experiences. When you tell your story, you're helping shape the way you are perceived and the way your culture works. You can help improve society by giving the gift of your personal experience. Whatever your medium is, tell your story.

Out of the Attic – Failure and Mistakes

You leap out the window and onto the roof of the attic. Standing on your right is a ghost in a cape and a top hat holding a hat box. His other hand holds a cane. His head, a fringe of hair sticking out on both sides, disappears from his shoulders and reappears in the box. There are hat boxes on a handcart in front of him, and lantern sits on a barrel. His ribs and leg bones are visible beneath the coat he wears. His shoes look like slip-ons. The ghost's head disappears form the box and reappears on his shoulders.

The Hatbox Ghost was the subject of rumors and legends. People who had experienced the Haunted Mansion when it first opened insisted that they had seen the ghost. Photographic evidence was scant if available at all. The Hatbox Ghost did exist, but it was removed because the effect didn't work. It was a failure.

"Failure is inevitable along the path to innovation" (Amabile and Kramer, p. 177). Creative people look at failure as a stepping stone to success. They use them as a lesson learned (Policastro and Gardner, p. 223). Whenever you start something new, you can expect there to be mistakes and failure. According to Eric Maisel, creativity is "a mistake making adventure" (p. 133).

These mistakes are only a problem if they are repeated or their lessons go unheeded. "Trust that you will make mistakes and plan on learning from them" (Nye, p. 140). Knowing that you'll make mistakes and fail ahead of time can prepare you to look for them and examine them while lessening the disappointment that comes with them.

"Human beings are the only creatures who are allowed to fail," said Author Madeleine L'Engle, "...We're allowed to learn from our mistakes and our failures. And that's how I learn..." (Csikszentmihalyi, 2013, p. 258). "There must be failure if we want to move forward," said Professor Gordon Wallace, "'Failure' is part of the programme to ensure progress" (McDonald, p. 117). "Failure can lead to greater competence when it becomes a basis for learning" (Fritz, p. 76).

Digital democracy expert Tiago Peixoto believes trial and error is the source of innovation (McDonald, p. 80). "Creation is a long journey where most turns are wrong and most ends are dead" (Ashton, p. 65). While creation and problem solving isn't often viewed in light of an "aha!" or "eureka!" moment, the anecdotes that support this type of theory are unsubstantiated or misunderstood when the whole process is examined.

"For innovation to flourish, one needs to recognize that it is important to fail," says author William Saito. "Failure is what drives innovation and is the necessary part of the 'innovation process.'" Saito defines innovation as the ability to learn from and build on failures (McDonald, p. 117).

"Failure is simply the opportunity to begin again more intelligently" (Henry Ford as cited in Amabile and Kramer, p. 177). In Imagineering, the Hatbox Ghost effect kept coming back. People would work on it in an attempt to make it right. In 2015, the Hatbox Ghost made his return for Disneyland's 60th anniversary, and he's laughed ever since.

    Ghosts fly up in front of you and you fall turning around to face the roof. Your descent is in slow motion as you come down past a brick chimney and through the trees that leer at you and grasp at you with their branches. A crow with red eyes caws at you, and you hit the ground. Stars shine in the night sky.

    The caretaker stands at the entrance to the graveyard. He holds up a lantern and shakes in his shoes. He is wearing a yellow scarf and holds a shovel in his left hand. He's the first living person you've seen since the hosts and hostesses that ushered you into the Doom Buggies, and he is scared witless. His half-starved dog stands next to him. The dog whines and quivers in fear. Strains of "Grim, Grinning Ghosts" can be heard from beyond the gate.

The Graveyard – At the Intersection

The gate attached to a brick column is open. On the right-hand side is a crypt and a gravestone. A spirit provides a jump scare here. The Doom Buggy spins to the left and you see a quintet of musicians playing along with the song "Grim, Grinning Ghosts." A ghost pops up from behind a nearby gravestone for a jump scare. A flautist sits in the coffin in front of the xylophonist, who appears to be a pirate. The xylophonist bangs away with two bones, probably femurs. The ghost playing the bagpipes is larger and wearing a pilgrim type hat. Next to him is a second pirate playing a harp, and a spirit with a feather in his cap is playing a horn. Two cats sit watching the quartet and two owls sit in the tree branches above. They stand in the midst of several graves. In the distance is a crypt and behind that ghostly forms are rising from the ground, an effect achieved with a mirror ball and projector.

A ghost wolf howls at the moon. All of the trees are bare. Two spirits use a see-saw and go up and down -- a king with his scepter, crown and pointy beard and a queen in her crown. The see-saw's fulcrum is a headstone. Another spirit in a princess hat sits on a swing behind them.

More ghosts rise from the ground, and the Doom Buggy swings back to the right to reveal five singing busts. Four are upright, one, rumored to be Walt Disney (but in fact, Thurl Ravenscroft), is broken at the neck and lies askew on his pedestal.

Turning back to the left, other spirits have joined the song. A gravestone moves up and down, behind it two spirits, a woman in a bonnet and a skinny man are having a picnic with a tablecloth and candelabra on a table and wine in a holder near them. A boney arm reaches out of a broken crypt and holds a glass of red drink in its hand. Behind them, ghosts ride bicycles around and around. A ghost head pops up for a jump scare.

A wagon-wheeled hearse with its coffin open and on the ground is next to the picnicking couple. The driver holding a horsewhip appears to be trying to help a woman down from the hearse. A teapot pours perpetually into a tea cup. A man sits, using the open coffin as a chair, drinking tea with another man that sits across from him. A popup ghost provides a jump scare from behind a headstone close to the Doom Buggy.

A starving dog, the same species as the caretaker's, looks at a mummy sitting in a coffin drinking tea. An old man with a long white beard stands next to the mummy. A horn in his ear and his constant "Eh?" "What's that?" and "Louder!" mark him as hard of hearing. Behind them is an Egyptian sarcophagus.

On the right side, the tombstones move and a crypt is open. A specter floats within; it's body and face covered in a cloak. A popup ghost provides a jump scare.

A pair of opera singers stand together. The skinny man is dressed in a knight's outfit with a sword. The proverbial fat lady complete with valkyrie helmet with wings, holds her clasped hands to her cheek and belts out the lyrics to "Grim, Grinning Ghosts." Next to them stands a man holding his own and his executioner with a huge axe. There are no hard feelings in the afterlife. A short, older man completes the trio while a boney arm and hand with a trowel sticks out of a brick wall. The trowel is dipping into the mortar. It will only take a couple more bricks for the spirit inside to be completely walled in. The red-eyed crow caws above you as the doom buggy glides into a crypt.

  The Spirits cross the boundary of space and time. They are at the intersection of life and death, and they come together from different time periods, different walks of life and different occupations. They all sing together. The Haunted Mansion itself is at the intersection of the park boundary as its show hall extends under the train and beyond the area that the guests are normally allowed. This attribute of disciplines coming together is accentuated during the holiday season from Halloween to Christmas when Jack and his friends from "The Nightmare before Christmas" take over the mansion and two holidays collide. Just like the different ghosts and holidays coming together at the Haunted Mansion in its holiday form and during other times of the year, "multiple components must converge for creativity to occur" (Sternberg and Lubart, p. 10).

  Creativity is often recognized as the combination of two or more ideas, and it often occurs when two fields intersect each other. According to Smith, Ward and Finke (p. 202), observers have noted that "synthesis or merging of previously separate concepts" is crucial to creativity, and creators recognize the ability to generate ideas through the consideration of "novel combinations of concepts."

Csikszentmihalyi notes that "useful new ideas are likely to arise from centers where people from different cultural backgrounds are able to interact and exchange ideas" (1999, p. 319). Creativity "involves crossing the boundaries of domains" (2013, p. 9).

"Koestler (1964) defines creativity in terms of the capacity to make connections – to bring together previously unconnected 'frames of reference'" (as cited in Nickerson, p. 394). The World Food Programme's Deputy Director Pierre Guillaume Wielezynski said "The more dots you see, the more connections you make... A curious mind that has the chance to experience different ideas, cultures and perspectives will inevitably think of new things" (McDonald, p. 92).

Scientist Linus Pauling said that he differs from other scientists because he brings "ideas from one field of knowledge into another field of knowledge" (Csikszentmihalyi, 2013, p. 118). Darwin knew about barnacles and animal breeding. Leonardo's knowledge of anatomy applied to his work as a sculptor. Newton made scientific instruments (as cited in Lavery, p. 23). Howard Gruber said that creative individuals "need to know a lot and cultivate special skills."

According to scientist Kary Mullis (as cited in Barron, Montuori and Barron, 1997), "important inventions almost always cross the lines of disciplines" (p. 70). "Moving between fields is the way to be creative" (p.73). Biologist Kary Mullis

(Barron, Montuori, and Barron, 1997, p. 70) said that "important inventions almost always cross the lines of disciplines."

As your Doom Buggy glides and spins its way through the graveyard, you can recognize the different fields and disciplines represented. They may be grouped together, but the graveyard allows for them to all be in one place, and when they aren't performing, they can intermingle and learn from each other. The friction created between the different cultures and characters will spark more creativity from them as they would in any diverse group.

If your workplace or life are filled with people who look, think and act like you and come from the same cultural background, you're missing out on one of the best ways to improve your creativity. Find ways to cultivate your knowledge and your social circle at the intersection and then find more intersections to cultivate.

Grim Grinning Ghosts – Teamwork

The song that dominates the Haunted Mansion is "Grim, Grinning Ghosts." With lyrics by X. Atencio and music by Buddy Baker, the song is the melodic strain that carries guests from the first scene to the last. Most notably sung by the busts in the graveyard, who make strange and disquieting faces as they sing, "Grim, Grinning Ghosts" is an anthem for creativity.

> "When the crypt doors creak and the tombstones quake,
> Spooks come out for a swinging wake.
> Happy haunts materialize and begin to vocalize.
> Grim grinning ghosts come out to socialize!
>
> Now, don't close your eyes and don't try to hide,
> For a silly spook may sit by your side.
> Shrouded in a daft disguise, they pretend to terrorize.
> Grim grinning ghosts come out to socialize!
>
> As the moon climbs high o'er the dead oak tree,
> Spooks arrive for the midnight spree.
> Creepy creeps with eerie eyes start to shriek and harmonize.
> Grim grinning ghosts come out to socialize!
>
> When you hear the knell of a requiem bell,
> Weird glows gleam where spirits dwell.

Restless bones etherealize, rise as spooks of every size!"

With its themes of happiness and grinning, "Grim, Grinning Ghosts" accentuates the positive, and optimism is curvilinearly correlated with creativity, which is to say that being optimistic will generally lead to greater creativity. The ghosts seem to come from nowhere, like ideas, the materialize. However, what stands out for "Grim Grinning Ghosts" is that it took a team to make the song, and it takes ghosts from everywhere to make the song as joyful as it is.

"Innovation doesn't happen through just one person; it's various people and various ideas from different backgrounds all fusing together into something that can actually be taken forward by the group," said Co-Founder of EyeNetra.com David Schafran (McDonald, p. 107).

Musician David Byrne says that collaboration is an aid to creativity; "I'll risk disaster because the creative rewards of a successful collaboration are great" (p. 199).

"Creativity is a collaborative process. Innovation comes from teams more often than from the lightbulb moments of lone geniuses" (Isaacson, p. 479).

"Almost all creation is a collaboration" (Barron, Montuori and Barron, 1997, p. 127).

It took the creative talents of people like Ken Anderson, X. Atencio, Claude Coats, Rolly Crump, Yale Gracey, Marc Davis, Thurl Ravenscroft, and Leota Toombs as well as the managerial talents of people like Walt Disney and Dick Nunis to bring the Haunted Mansion to life. The team of imagineers and those who built the structure wouldn't have worked as well if one person had been missing.

"Grim, Grinning Ghosts" was also a collaborative effort. Walt Disney encouraged X. Atencio, who had no song writing experience, to write the theme for the Pirates of the Caribbean attraction. Atencio didn't consider himself a song writer, but "Yo Ho (A Pirate's Life for Me)" became a classic. Atencio teamed with Buddy Baker and proved the first song was no fluke.

Walt Disney said, "It seems shallow and arrogant for anyone in these times to claim that he is completely self-made and that he owes all his success to his own unaided efforts." The individual is a part of the success, but "many hands and hearts and minds generally contribute to anyone's notable achievements" (Kurtti, 2008, p. xii).

Marc Davis believes that he supplied most of the ideas for the Haunted Mansion, but the attraction "was done in a kind of group decision process" (Kurtti, 2008, p. 52).

"Ah, there you are, and just in time. There's a little matter I forgot to mention: Beware of hitchhiking ghosts," says the Ghost Host, and he laughs.

The Crypt – Travel

The hitchhiking ghosts have there thumbs out and are pointed in the direction you're going. The larger one wears a top hat and vest with coat and tie. He carries a carpet bag. The tall skinny one is skeletal. His sardonic grin doesn't help him seem friendlier. He doffs his cap in greeting revealing his bald head with fringe of hair around the edges. The third one is short and has a long beard. He holds a ball that is attached to his ankle by a chain. Their clothes are transparent allowing glimpses of the skeletons underneath.

"They have selected you to fill our quota, and they'll haunt you until you return! Now I will raise the safety bar, and a ghost will follow you home!" The Ghost Host laughs.

When Walt Disney assigned Ken Anderson to the project in 1957, Anderson "started by visiting haunted houses in Louisiana" (Gennawey, p. 129). He went north to San Jose to visit the Winchester Mystery House. Travel informed the stories that Anderson proposed for the mansion and included a notorious pirate, whose naïve bride learns his identity. The pirate kills her and she haunts him until he commits suicide.

In 1958, Disney was in London giving an interview, and he mentioned that he was building haunted house for all of the ghosts that were being displaced by a modernizing England. This idea for a retirement home was used by Marty Sklar when he drafted an announcement that was posted outside of the Haunted Mansion in 1963.

Traveling to a place where the people involved in a particular field congregate improves your opportunity to learn more about your field while interacting with the experts and finding opportunities to move forward with your own creative efforts. Actors go to Hollywood. Artists go to New York (Csikszentmihalyi, 2013, p. 128). If you want to engage in oceanography, it helps to live near an ocean; Alaska, Hawaii, and Monterey, CA, are all places you may decide to go.

Interaction is important for creative stimulation (Csikszentmihalyi, 2013, p. 129). If you live in a small town or are isolated from the people in your field and others who can stimulate thinking, travel can get you to a place that will spark new ideas.

"I like to travel personally, and that's a good way to expand horizons and find new things you want to do" says author Brian C. Baer (2017).

Some places are conducive to refilling your creative well. According to Csikszentmihalyi, "Pliny the Younger, Leonardo da Vinci, and the poets Giuseppe Parini and Ippolito Nievo" chose the village of Bellagio as their place to replenish their creativity as did Franz Liszt (2013, p. 134).

Artist Herb Ryman opened a gallery in 1932 that he said didn't have a single person come into it during the few months it was opened. When he closed it, he traveled through the southwestern United States. "Everywhere I looked, the variety of nature's forms and materials excited and fed the soul of this anxious artist," said Ryman (Kurtti, 2008, p. 10). After a couple of years at MGM, Ryman traveled the world again to get away from the phoniness of motion pictures. During his time abroad, he created art that was showcased at Chouinard Art Institute and got him a job with The Disney Company (Kurtti, 2008, p. 11).

    The Doom Buggy turns to left and into a hall of mirrors. The mirrors are large enough to reflect the open portion of the buggy. They are oval, ornately framed and hanging from a rope attached to them at two opposite points of the frame. As you pass, each mirror reflects you in the buggy with the ghost that has decided to go home with you in the center of the Doom Buggy.

The Exit – Humor

You exit the mirror hall, and the safety bar on the Doom Buggy pops open.

"Please exit to your left by stepping away from the cars with your left foot first. Step out and stand on the moving platform," a woman says.

Stepping out with your left foot onto the moving platform, there is a wrought iron fence blocking off a mausoleum that has been set underground. Roots encroach on the individual sections. A skeletal arm in the wall holds a torch to dimly light the area. You are carried to the transitional walkway.

"Please exit by stepping away from the cars with your left foot first. Step out and stand on the moving platform, please," says a male voice.

A ghostly group sings overhead. "If would like to join our jamboree, there's a simple rule that's compulsory. Mortals pay a token fee. Rest in peace, the haunting's free. So, hurry back, we would like your company."

The transitional walkway has a trash can next to another moving platform that goes upwards. You get on this platform and go up. Your feet stray close to the edge, and you feel rollers under them as if it is intended for a foot massage. On the left is an alcove, and a tiny figure in a wedding dress speaks to the crowd as you move by. She is standing on the far side of what may be an ornate fireplace mantle. The closest platform to the bottom of the walkway is empty, the middle platform has a dead plant on it.

"Hurry back! Hurry back! Be sure to bring your death certificate if you decide to join us. Make final arrangements now! We've been dying to have you."

At the end of the walkway are a couple of turnstiles. Turning to the left, you go out the door between two brick walls. You hear a sinister laugh behind you. It appears the Haunted Mansion has had the last laugh.

Even in development of the Haunted Mansion, Rolly Crump and Yale Gracey looked for the humor. They were told that they needed to leave the light on in their work area because the janitors didn't want to go in when it was dark. With magic and ghost effects everywhere, it was just too scary. Crump and Gracey left the lights on, but rigged the room with an infrared tripwire. When the janitor came in, the lights went off, the blacklight and all of the ghost effects came on. The next morning, they found a broom in the middle of the floor and were told they would need to clean the room themselves. The janitors wouldn't go in anymore (Surrell, 2015, p. 18).

Bill Nye said that when you're able to find the humor of a situation, you're able to step outside your normal viewpoint. It's this shift that allows you change perspectives and find new solutions (p. 144). Punning connects concepts and domains you wouldn't normally put together. It allows you to play at the intersection and trains your brain for "conceptual flexibility" (p. 146).

"Humor and 'sense of humor' are basically creative and are themselves facilitative of further creativity" (Torrance, p. 188).

Marc Davis brought humor to the Jungle Cruise, the Pirates of the Caribbean, the Mine Train through Nature's Wonderland, and the Haunted Mansion. His sight gags and staging are among the qualities that make the Haunted Mansion the classic attraction it is.

You go through the gates and return to the world of the living. And hopefully, after reading this book, you'll have returned to the world of the truly living, those who tap into their creative drive and use it to make the world better through beauty, joy, and better problem solving. Thank you.

Afterword: Memories from Mom
By Celia Wallis,

When I was asked to write up a special memory of the Haunted Mansion at Disneyland, I thought, "Oh, there are so many". I would take my children every year to Disneyland as our family vacation. I found Disneyland was always a special place where we would forget any issues or problems for the four or five days we spent there. So, I have many, many memories.

I can share one of our most memorable experiences on the Haunted Mansion. Part of the experience of this ride is to be able to wait in the line and read all the head stones on the pathway. There are two sides so lots to read. Sometimes, the kids would make something up that sounded pretty funny.

Then we go into the Mansion to a room that gets dark, and the walls close in, I always reached for the two to make sure no ghost took them away in the dark. My son would recite the words in a deep voice mimicking the voice from the speakers. My daughter would let off the highest pitch scream. Down we go and magically, the doors open, so we follow a hall to find the Omnimover to join the spirits' party.

The kids would walk and jump in, and I would move as quickly as a mom can and kind of fall into the middle of the two of them. We always laughed at my agility. Then the song would play, we had been on the ride so many times we could sing to it. My son knew all the words, and he would do it with animation.

One of my daughter's favorite scenes was Madame Leota, whose head was in a round glass dome, she would haunt us with her threats of calling in the spirits before we could leave. The boney dogs, the spirits trying to escape from the casket or from behind locked doors, the bride who never was, and always a happy singing fivesome.

Of course, we always ended up with some hitchhikers catching a ride in our Omnimover, at which we would all scream and laugh. The spirit party must have enjoyed our company because we were always invited back when "we get our death certificate!"

Celia Wallis is a Disney enthusiast, emergency room nurse, mom, and my hero.

Practical Guide to Improving Creativity
Have a goal.

Creativity is often depicted as a free-wheeling process where anything goes. During idea generation, this might be true. However, more often, people use creativity to solve a particular problem or come up with ideas to use in a project. Having a goal sets the parameters of the creativity that paradoxically enhance a person's ability to become more creative.

Write it down.

Ideas come and go. They enter the mind, and unless they are given attention, they leave. Sometimes, they never return. Make sure that doesn't happen to you. Write it down. Record it. Make notes in a way that you can review them regularly.

Play.

Play comes naturally to people. Use it to your advantage and start playing with everything. Play with your words, play with your tools, play with your children, and play with ideas. Play facilitates creativity. Have a playful attitude and become more creative.

Fill the well.

No matter what you do, you need to take a break. This is true for your creativity. You need to fill the well and replenish your creative reserves so you don't stagnate and can continue to create. Whatever it takes to help keep you creating, make time for it before you burnout. Filling the well is different for everyone, and it may include meditation, movies, travel, concerts, or reading a good book.

Keep learning.

The more you learn, the more dots you'll have to connect. Learning something new allows you to develop new skills and new perspectives. It also allows you to find where different domains or subject matters come together. Be a lifelong learner and watch your creativity soar.

Expect rejection.

Any time you come up with something new, you will be faced with people who don't like change, no matter how good it is for them. Rather than accepting your new idea, they will do their best to undermine it. It will be outright rejected. People will throw up obstacles related to identity, beliefs and other reasons that you won't even consider. Expecting rejection allows you to keep your spirits up while fighting for your idea. If your idea is accepted without rejection, you can be pleasantly surprised.

Get comfortable.

If nowhere else, you need to be in a comfortable head space to create. That means removing worries over bills, dealing with the kids and spouse, figuring out what's wrong with your health and any other everyday worry you might encounter. For the time that you're creating, you need to be okay with where you are and work in the moment. Knowing that you're in a safe place to create will allow you to do so. By being comfortable when you begin, you can do the uncomfortable things that come with creating.

Take a risk.

You'll be facing failure, mistakes and possible ridicule. If you want to be more creative, you're going to have to take a risk. Take small ones first if that helps you build your risk tolerance.

Carry the process further.

Most people find a solution that works, and they stop there. However, when you carry the process further, you can find better solutions that solve more than just the problem at hand. IN the case of a project like a theme park, you may be able to "plus" your projects and make them better by being more creative, more often.

Find and be a mentor.

A good way to learn is through the use of a mentor. By finding someone who has experience in the skills that you want, you can get tips and hints that you would never find in a book or on a YouTube video. More importantly, you can ask questions and learn in a manner that's appropriate to your style. Becoming a mentor offers you the same experience from the other side. If you want to keep your skills fresh and learn something new or better, teaching it helps a lot. Become a mentor for someone from a different socio-economic, cultural background, and you'll have an amazing opportunity to become more creative and better at your core skills.

Practice.

Like any skill, there are people who are more creative than you. However, when creativity comes naturally some people will eschew practice and rely on their talent to get by. With practice, you can improve your creativity and the tools that you use to become more creative. Do something for your creativity every day and watch your skills grow as you mind embraces flexibility in thought and action.

Stretch your imagination.

The imagination is the combining element of the mind that is the basis for all of creativity. It takes all of the inputs that you've learned and remembered and allows you to access them in a different way. Stretch your imagination regularly by reading fantasy and science fiction or other fiction books outside of your regular reading. Write down your dreams. Create stories, even if they aren't meant for anyone else to read. Join a role-playing game and play weekly. Tell stories you make up to your children

Embrace Change.

Change is scary, but it's always constant. By embracing change, you can take the fear out of it and improve your ability to direct and prepare for it. Change is often good. Embrace it.

Change Your Perspective.

In order to find new ways of doing, you need to find new ways of seeing. People tend to take the same literal and figurative point of view into every situation. You can change this by changing your position, literally: Get down on the ground, stand on your head, only look at something with your non-dominant eye, or stand on (an OSHA approved) chair.

You can change your point of view figuratively by imagining you're another person, like Leonardo da Vinci or like a firefighter; you could also imagine yourself as a flower, a giraffe, or an inanimate object, like a pencil or car. Then ask yourself how this person, animal, plant or object would approach the problem.

Tolerate ambiguity.

You won't know where you're going when you start a new creative project. You might have a general direction and a goal, but how you get there and what the actual outcomes will be are still undecided. By tolerating ambiguity, you won't get stuck in second-guessing or over-analyzing. It's okay to wander; it doesn't mean you're lost.

Keep the ideas flowing.

Idea generation is the first step to being creative. The More ideas you have, the more likely you are to find a great idea that you can go forward with. Idea generation helps break blocks and keeps you moving in the right direction. Allow the ideas to flow freely throughout the creative process and be sure to capture those ideas.

Be curious.

Curiosity is a powerful asset in all areas of your life. You won't just accept memes or wild accusations; you'll follow through and find out the real story. As long as you have a way to verify your findings and curtail your confirmation bias, your curiosity will help you explore avenues that others won't go down. That exploration will help you be more creative.

Believe you can.

The first thing you need to be more creative is to believe you can become more creative. You were creative once; you can be creative again. You just have to believe in yourself first.

Have courage.

There are a lot of barriers to being creative. You have to have the courage to overcome those barriers. Whether you're afraid people will reject you or you don't want to share your ideas because of ridicule, you need courage to do so. Creativity can be just about your own enjoyment and self-fulfillment; however, by showing your creative efforts, you're allowing others to become more creative. Have the courage to do the work, follow through with it and share it.

Make time.

Life is busy, and it won't slow down. You need to carve time out of your busy schedule to be creative. Put it on your calendar. Make sure your family knows how important it is, and guard that time jealously. Some creators get up at 4:30 am because no one else is awake. Others stay awake until 2 am. You don't have to do either of these, but you do need to find a time where you can work uninterrupted.

Create synergy.

Think about all the activities you do and figure out how they can enhance each other. For writers, taking research for a book or story and turning it into a blog post for fans is an easy act of synergy where you take the work you do and allow it to perform more than it would otherwise do. This will generate buzz around the book and sell more copies. How synergy works for you will be different.

Create a stimulating environment.

You won't always be able to travel or change your venue. If you create a space that helps you remember your adventures and the things you've done that were different from a normal day, you'll be better able to draw from your experiences. Improve on that with anything that you find inspiring, possibly using a corkboard you can change frequently, and you'll have a winning environment that will support your creative endeavors.

Make something old new again.

Finding a new use for an old item is one way to be creative. By repurposing an object or idea you already have, you're practicing combining different elements that didn't go together before. Old technology can be a great place to start for creativity. Be sure to do your research first.

Tell your story.

You have a story different from anyone else in the world. If you don't tell it in your way, the world won't get the benefits of it. You can choose the medium for your story, but be sure to tell it for your posterity and for the world.

Fail and learn from it.

Failure is the stepping stone to greater creativity. When you're doing something new, you will fail. It's what you do with that failure that's important. As Walt said, "I think it's important to have a good hard failure when you're young. I learned a lot out of that."

Make mistakes and learn from them.

You're going to make mistakes. As long as you learn from them, it's okay, even if you only learn what not to do next time.

Go to the intersection.

Creativity happens at the point where two disciplines collide, much like the Haunted Mansion Holiday, where two holidays collide. Learning and thinking deeply about different subjects will help you find the intersections that can help you create something new.

Work as a team.

Having someone to work with can come in different forms. Maybe you have a partner, like Roy O. Disney who does the finances and let's you work the more creative side. (Roy was creative in his own right, even if popular opinion doesn't hold that to be true. Roy's ability to find money for Walt's projects took creativity, too.) Maybe you have someone you can bounce an idea off of. You might be a writer who works with an artist. Teams come in different forms. What's important is to team with positive people who are also creative.

Travel.

Traveling introduces you to different ways of living and seeing the world. Be sure to get out of your comfort zone when you travel. Don't just hit the tourist spots with your tour guide. Instead, try to find ways to delve deeply into the culture. It worked for Herb Ryman, who spent time in Asia. It'll help you, too.

Use humor.

Edward de Bono says that humor does the same thing that creativity does. It takes you in one direction and then suddenly veers of in another direction that is logical in hindsight. Using humor allows you to play with situations and words while lowering your inhibitions and taking you to new situations. Have fun, use humor and reduce the stress that limits your creativity.

Disneyland Glossary and Other Terms

This section presents the key terms as defined for the purpose of this study. It includes a number of definitions as a result of the review of the pertinent literature and other key terms relevant to the study.

Attractions: Rides and shows at Disneyland.

Audio-animatronics: The name for the performers in the park that are made of electronics. The first audio-animatronics were the birds at the Enchanted Tiki Room. Disneyland also has a President Abraham Lincoln, pirates, dinosaurs and several other creatures that qualify as audio-animatronics.

Berm: A construction term describing a mound of dirt that surrounds an area.

Blue Sky Thinking: The Disney term for coming up with ideas without judgement or worry about resources.

Cast Members: The people who work at Disneyland. While they are at the park in view of guests, they are On Stage. While they are at work but not in view of the guests, they are Off Stage or Back Stage.

Creativity: The application of imagination to come up with something new. That something may be tangible, like a new product or service, or it may be something whimsical that only has value to its creator.

Everyday Creativity: The processes and ideas that may or may not lead to new products or services but do lead to the joy of discovery and allows a person to more fully realize his or her personhood. It is important to note that this concept of everyday creativity is extended to people who have jobs that are considered creative. Borrowing from Csikszentmihalyi (2013), this creativity does not necessarily include extraordinary creativity that changes a domain but rather it focuses on the individual achievement of creativity for oneself and one's immediate area.

Guests: Visitors to Disneyland.

Illusioneering: Using magic and tricks to create a new source of entertainment. Imagineering with the use of illusions.

Imagineers: The people who work for the Disney Company that are responsible for generating and developing ideas for the theme park attractions.

Innovation: The application of creativity that leads to something tangible like a new product, service or way of doing something.

Lands at Disneyland include Main Street, U.S.A., Adventureland, New Orleans Square, Frontierland, Fantasyland, Tomorrowland, Mickey's Toon Town and Critter

Country. Each land is themed and anachronisms produced by the Disney Company and its employees are seldom tolerated. (For example, a spaceman in Frontierland wouldn't happen, again.)

Metaphor: A way of relating one domain to another so that the less familiar domain is more easily understood. Metaphors, according to language scholars, do not use comparison words. However, people will often refer to a comparison colloquially as a metaphor even when "like" or "as" are used.

Queue: A line people stand in, usually to get to an attraction or food.

WED: The name for the Imagineering department when it was first developed; taken from the initials of Walter Elias Disney.

Weenie: The word that Walt used to describe a feature that sparked curiosity enough to lead people toward it. Legend has it that he noticed he could get his dog to do anything if he dangled out a weenie. Adventureland is the only land without a weenie though Tomorrowland has arguably moved its current weenie to the front of the land.

The Characters of the Haunted Mansion

This list only includes the characters in Disneyland's Haunted Mansion and its lore. It does not include any characters from any of the other versions of the Haunted Mansion or from the movie. It does contain some of the character descriptions that were created and discarded during the process of bringing the attraction to life:

Master Gracey: The owner of the house, may also be in the portrait gallery where he changes into a skeleton.

Ghost Host: The narrator, who is sometimes mistaken for Master Gracey. He hangs himself from the rafters in the stretching room.

The Raven: Appears several times throughout the ride.

Madame Z, a full-bodied clairvoyant in a 1964 version by Marc Davis.

Madame Leota: She has a remarkable head for materializing the disembodied.

Anthony and Cleopatra: Considered as part of the 999 happy haunts.

Great Caesar's Ghost: In the ballroom scene.

Pickwick on the chandelier in the ballroom.

Granny in the rocking chair in the ballroom.

Ghostly Bride, the first version she had a glowing red heart that thumped in the attic.

Constance the Killer Bride, the new version. She's a black widow bride who gains wealth, as indicated by her strands of pearls in each wedding portrait, with every husband she beheads.

Gus, Ezra, Phineas - the hitchhiking ghosts.

Bloodmere Manor: One of the proposed names for the Haunted Mansion.

Captain Bartholomew Gore, Captain Gideon Gorelieu, Black Bart, Gore Mansion.

Priscilla Gore, the ill-fated wife.

Monsieur Bogyman and Mlle. Vampire: Many different monsters, including some from Universal were originally considered during the idea generating phase for the Haunted Mansion.

Dracula.

Frankenstein.

Headless Horseman: From Disney's "The Legend of Sleepy Hollow."

Walt Disney: Considered as a host for the attraction; he would've been a projection version of himself.

Lonesome Ghost: Would have acted as the Ghost Host.

Hairy the Arm: Trying to grab the guides from behind.

Hat Box Ghost at debut and then 2015.

Little Leota: the Ghostess portrayed by Leota Toombs at the attraction's exit.

The Organ from 20,000 Leagues under the Sea (1954).

Beauregard the Butler: A guide.

Uncle Theodore: Thurl Ravenscroft bust.

Phineas P. Pock: Singing bust with face and voice of Bob Ebright.

Ned Nub: Singing bust with face and voice of Jay Mayer.

Rollo Rumpkin: Singing bust with face and voice of Verne Rowe.

Cousin Algernon: Singing bust with face and voice of Chuck Schroeder.

The busts are also known as "the Phantom Five."

Alexander Nitrokoff on the barrel in the stretching gallery.

Widow Abigail Patecleaver killed George as featured in a painting in the stretching gallery.

Grand Hall Duelists.

Constance's husbands: Ambrose, Frank, the Marquis, Reginald and George.

The Creators of the Haunted Mansion

While WED, or Walt Disney Imagineering, is responsible for the creation of the Haunted Mansion, and no one printed resource could possibly explore the contributions of everyone who worked to bring the Haunted Mansion to life. I will try to highlight as many of the people who were involved with its creation as possible. The creators in this section are listed in no particular order.

If you want to know more about Walt Disney and his creativity, read Bob Thomas' "An American Original." It is the seminal biography of Walt Disney. You can also check out an article I wrote at penguinate.com (https://penguinate.weebly.com/walt-disney-and-creativity.html) and included in "Penguinate! The Disney Company," for a very short amount of information on Walt Disney and his creativity.

Ken Anderson was the first imagineer assigned to develop the ideas for the Haunted Mansion. He traveled to the south and to the Winchester Mystery House during his research.

Yale Gracey was the imagineering tinkerer Walt gave leeway to do whatever he wanted.

Rolly Crump worked with Gracey and came up with a collection of ideas so disturbing that Walt thought about them all night. Those items were going to be a part of the Museum of the Weird, but the museum never materialized.

Ed Kohn worked on the changing portraits.

Blaine Gibson was the master sculptor at the Disney Company. He's responsible for Abraham Lincoln, the pirates of Pirates of the Caribbean and many of the ghosts in the Haunted Mansion. Gibson has also sculpted the Partners statue at the Hub

Wathel Rogers helped pioneer audio-animatronics.

Paul Frees is the voice of the Ghost Host.

Ken Chapman helped design the attraction's poster.

Marc Davis was the humorist who came up with the funny spirits of the Haunted Mansion.

Harriet Burns, the first female imagineer, did models for the Haunted Mansion.

Claude Coats provided the atmosphere of the Haunted Mansion and looked for the attraction to be scary.

Ub Iwerks came up with a projection technique similar to the one that Yale Gracey and Rolly Crump created for the Madame Leota effect.

Leota Toombs was an imagineer who is the face of Madame Leota and the face and voice of Little Leota. She is also the mother of Kim Irvine.

Dick Irvine took over management of the Haunted Mansion attraction after Walt's death.

Dick Nunis was the Disneyland executive who required that the ride become a "people eater."

Harper Goff was the second imagineer according to Jeff Kurtti (2015, p. 2). [Walt Disney was the first.] Goff drew the first concept art of a haunted house for a Disney park.

Marvin Davis worked on earlier concepts for the Haunted Mansion's location before New Orleans Square.

Sam McKim worked on concepts related to New Orleans Square.

Marty Sklar created a sign, inspired by an interview Walt Disney did, that created anticipation for the attraction long before it opened.

X. Atencio wrote the script for the attraction and the lyrics to "Grim, Grinning Ghosts."

Buddy Baker composed the music for X. Atencio's "Grim, Grinning Ghosts" lyrics. He also changed the music to fit the scenes in the Haunted Mansion and included the use of detuned instruments to make them sound creepier.

The Mellomen are the singers who can be found in the graveyard as busts come to life.

Thurl Ravenscroft is the most famous of the Mellomen and is often mistaken for Walt Disney in the attraction. Ravenscroft also did the voice for the Grinch and Tony the Tiger because he's great!

Wayne Jackson helped develop audio-animatronics.

Roger Broggie helped develop audio-animatronics.

Bill Justice programmed the audio-animatronics.

Bob Baranick encouraged the purchase of the hearse.

Tony Baxter hitched the horse to the hearse.

Eleanor Audley provide the voice of Madame Leota. She was also Lady Tremaine in "Cinderella" and Maleficent in "Sleeping Beauty."

Chris Turner drew up the floating Leota effect.

Kim Irvine provided Leota's face for Holiday Haunted Mansion and came up with the idea for the pet cemetery. She is the daughter of Leota Toombs.

Chris Goosman created the story for Constance the Black Widow Bride and came up with the epitaphs for the first pet cemetery.

Julia Lee is the body of Constance, and Kat Cressida is her voice.

Chris Runco provided some concept art for the Haunted Mansion.

Resources and Bibliography

Not all of these books or other materials were used for quote material. Some were consulted as part of the research but not directly used in the writing of this book. Still, I enjoyed the books, and they should be a part of anyone's library.

Aitken, Brian. *Making of The Haunted Mansion (Part 1 of 2)* (2007A). https://youtu.be/vzEFQ4idTRM

Aitken, Brian. *Making of The Haunted Mansion (Part 2 of 2)* (2007B). https://youtu.be/XHdvZpDwBrM

Alexander, KM. "Author KM Alexander on creativity" interview with Shad Engkilterra at Lilac City Comicon (2017). https://youtu.be/EoIzJLULFJM

Amabile, Teresa and Kramer, Steven. *The Progress Principle: Using Small Wins to Ignite Joy, Engagement, and Creativity at Work* (2011). Harvard Business Review Press, Boston, MA.

Ashton, Kevin. *How to Fly a Horse: The Secret History of Creation, Invention, and Discovery* (2015). Anchor Books, New York.

Barron, Frank, Montuori, Alfonso and Barron, Anthea. *Creators on Creating: Awakening and Cultivating the Imaginative Mind* (1997). Jeremy P. Tarcher/Putnam, New York.

Baer, Brian C. "Writer Brian C Baer on creativity" interview with Shad Engkilterra at Lilac City Comicon (2017). https://youtu.be/cTI76FwYB9Q

Baham, Jeff. *The Unauthorized Story of Walt Disney's Haunted Mansion* (2014). Theme Park Press.

Beard, Alison. "Maya Angelou on Courage and Creativity" in *The Harvard Business* Review, May (2013). https://hbr.org/2013/05/maya-angelou-on-courage-and-cr

Beard Institute. The Ultimate Mustache Guide: Grooming, Trimming, Shaping and More (2014). https://beardinstitute.com/beard-grooming/mustache-guide/

Bloomston, Carrie. *The Little Spark: 30 Ways to Ignite Your Creativity* (2014). Stash Books, Lafayette, CA.

Bundy, Travis. "Artist Travis Bundy on creativity" interview with Shad Engkilterra at Lilac City Comicon (2018). https://youtu.be/bbqO6R9O2is

Byrne, David. *How Music Works* (2017). Three Rivers Press, New York.

Castellano, Stephanie. "The Ancient Roots of Disney's Blockbuster Film 'Frozen'" (2014). Antiquity Now. https://antiquitynow.org/2014/06/03/the-ancient-roots-of-disneys-blockbuster-film-frozen/

Chartgeek.com. Movember Beard Styles (2013). https://www.chartgeek.com/movember-beard-styles/

Choi, Jin Nam, Anderson, Troy A., and Veillette, Anick. *Group & Organization Management* Vol. 34 No. 3 "Contextual Inhibitors of Employee Creativity in Organizations: The Insulating Role of Creative Ability (June, 2009) p. 330 to 357. Sage Publications. https://journals.sagepub.com/doi/pdf/10.1177/1059601108329811

Christopher, Brianne. "Explaining the Pepper's Ghost Illusion with Ray Optics" (2016). Comsol Blog. https://www.comsol.com/blogs/explaining-the-peppers-ghost-illusion-with-ray-optics/

Congdon, Lisa. *Art Inc.: The Essential Guide for Building Your Career as an Artist* (2014). Chronicle Books, San Francisco.

Csikszentmihalyi, Mihaly. "Implications of a Systems Perspective for the Study of Creativity" in the Handbook of Creativity (1999). Cambridge University Press, U.S.

Csikszentmihalyi, Mihaly. *Creativity: The Psychology of Discovery and Invention* (2013). Harper Perennial Modern Classics, New York.

D23. Disneyland's Pet Cemetery (accessed 2018). https://d23.com/d23-presents-disneylands-pet-cemetery/

Dahl, Roald. *The Witches* (2013). Puffin Books, Great Britain.

Daveland. Disneyland Haunted Mansion Photo Page: Line Queue (2006). https://www.davelandweb.com/hauntedmansion/index.html#petcemetery

De Bono, Edward. Talk at the Edward de Bono Institute, 2015. University of Malta, Malta.

Disney Parks Scripts. Haunted Mansion (Disneyland) (2017). http://www.disneyparkscripts.com/haunted-mansion-disneyland/

Demetriou, Christopher. "Writer Chris talks about creativity at Malta Comic Con 2015" interview with Shad Engkilterra. https://youtu.be/HIf6FNF9Mg4

DoomBuggies.com. Secrets of the Haunted Mansion: The Foyer and Gallery (accessed 2018). http://www.doombuggies.com/secrets_foyer.php

DoomBuggies.com. Secrets of the Haunted Mansion: The Grand Hall (accessed 2018). http://www.doombuggies.com/secrets_ballroom2.php

Dyson, Tony. "R2-D2 builder Tony Dyson talks play and creativity at Malta Comic Con 2015" interview with Shad Engkilterra (2015). https://youtu.be/3DDGGv8_pdg

Ealy, C. Diane. *The Woman's Book of Creativity* (1995). Beyond Words Publishing, Hillsboro, Oregon.

Engkilterra, Shad. *Disneyland Is Creativity: 25 Tips for Becoming More Creative* (2017). Shad Engkilterra, Canada.

Fanning, Jim. *The Disney Book: A Celebration of the World of Disney* (2015). DK Penguin Random House, New York.

Fenech, Dean. "Dean Fenech talks creativity at Malta Comic Con 2015" interview with Shad Engkilterra (2015). https://youtu.be/4KodUNQ_LOE

Freedogshampoo. *Imagineering Department - The Haunted Mansion* (2007). https://youtu.be/NgsA3v56gGg

Fritz, Robert. *Creating* (1991). Fawcett Columbine, New York.

Gennawey, Sam. *The Disneyland Story: The Unofficial Guide to the Evolution of Walt Disney's Dream* (2014). Keen Communications, Birmingham, Alabama.

Gentry, Cynthia. "Play and Creativity" (2015). http://www.importanceofplay.eu/blog/article/play-and-creativity

Gruber, Howard E. and Wallace, Doris B. "The Case Study Method and Evolving Systems Approach for Understanding Unique Creative People at Work" in the *Handbook of Creativity* (1999). Cambridge University Press, U.S.

Hahn, Don. *Brain Storm: Unleashing Your Creative Self* (2011). Disney Editions, New York.

HDThrillSeeker. Haunted Mansion ride at Disneyland - HDThrillSeeker (2012). https://youtu.be/eOJdC_7vlus

Higuchi, Takeo. The Idea Marathon workshop at the Edward de Bono Institute (2014). University of Malta, Malta.

Isaacson, Walter. *The Innovators: How a Group of Hackers, Geniuses and Geeks Created the Digital Revolution* (2014). Simon and Schuster, London.

Karstens Creations. Disney's Haunted Mansion Ballroom How It's Done (2013). https://youtu.be/fAryLSRcub0

Kashdan, Todd. *Curious? Discover the Missing Ingredient to a Fulfilling Life* (2009). William Morrow, New York.

Korkis, Jim. Mouseplanet.com. *Ken Anderson's Haunted Mansions Part One* (2014). https://www.mouseplanet.com/10786/Ken_Andersons_Haunted_Mansions_Part_One

Kurtti, Jeff. *Walt Disney's Imagineering Legends and the Genesis of the Disney Theme Park* (2008). Disney Editions, New York.

Langridge, Roger. "How to be more creative with cartoonist Roger Langridge" interview with Sahd Engkilterra at Malta Comic Con (2016). https://youtu.be/HjdeRiW9bBo

Lavery, David. *Joss Whedon, a Creative Portrait: From Buffy the Vampire Slayer to Marvel's The Avengers* (2014). I.B. Tauris & Co., New York.

LMGVids. *[HD]Best Low Light 2015 Haunted Mansion Disneyland Full Complete Ridethrough POV* (2015). https://youtu.be/WsQtKkRE8ss

Lubart, Todd I. "Creativity Across Cultures" in the *Handbook of Creativity* (1999). Cambridge University Press, U.S.

McDonald, Kim Chandler. *Innovation: How innovators think, act and change our world* (2013). Kogan Page, Great Britain.

McLean, S. (Producer), & Lynch, P. (Director). *The Ray Bradbury Theatre* (1989). United States: Echo Bridge. https://youtu.be/2nIqGI5-6HI

Magro, Peter and Peschel, Ashley. "How to be more creative with the writer and artist for S.T.E.A.M. at Malta Comic Con 2015" interview with Shad Engkilterra (2015). https://youtu.be/am_cvVPlvfQ

Maisel, Eric. *Fearless Creating: A Step-by-Step Guide to Starting and Completing Your Work of Art* (1995). Jeremy P. Tarcher and Putnam Book, New York.

Merrill, Carrie. "Author Carrie Merrill on creativity" interview with Shad Engkilterra at Lilac City Comicon (2017). https://youtu.be/R1SqYB_eAkQ

Meyers, Jonboy. "Artist Jonboy Meyers on creativity" interview with Shad Engkilterra at Lilac City Comicon (2017). https://youtu.be/bkOkqkGr4ko

Nickerson, Raymond S. "Enhancing Creativity" in the *Handbook of Creativity* (1999). Cambridge University Press, U.S.

Nye, Bill. *Everything All At Once* (2017). Rodale Books, New York.

Oh My Disney. Let's Take a Tour of the Haunted Mansion Graveyard (accessed 2018). https://ohmy.disney.com/news/2013/10/26/lets-take-a-tour-of-the-haunted-mansion-graveyard/

Park Ride History. *The History of & Changes to The Haunted Mansion | Disneyland* (2017). https://youtu.be/nPLgL_hGQ1M

Policastro, E. and Gardner, H. "From Case Studies to Robust Generalizations: An Approach to the Study of Creativity" in the *Handbook of Creativity* (1999). Cambridge University Press, U.S.

Questlove and Greenman, Ben. *Creative Quest* (2018). Ecco, New York.

Schellekens, Jasper. "The creative process and how to be more creative with School of Bitches Jasper" interview with Shad Engkilterra at Malta Comic Con (2015). https://youtu.be/oU2raN256KA

Scully, Daniel. "Artist Daniel Scully on creativity" interview with Shad Engkilterra at Lilac City Comicon (2017). https://youtu.be/IILxUx_KHAQ

Serling, Anne. *As I Knew Him: My Dad, Rod Serling* (2013). Citadel Press Books, New York.

Shepherd, Blacky. "Artist Blacky Shepherd on creativity" interview with Shad Engkilterra at Lilac City Comicon (2017). https://youtu.be/h2CpepQi5m8

Smith, Greg and Tanner, Michael. "Greg Smith and Michael Tanner of Junior Braves of the Apocalypse on Creativity" interview with Shad Engkilterra at Lilac City Comicon (2018). https://youtu.be/4NZKcl03rC4

SoCal Theme Parks 360. [Ultra HD] Haunted Mansion Ride Ultra Clarity POV at Disneyland Resort (2013). https://youtu.be/y-HC_tpveyo

SoCal Theme Parks 360. [EXTREME Low Light] FULL Haunted Mansion Ride-Through POV - Disneyland (2015). https://youtu.be/xCi1F0bu598

SoCal Theme Parks 360. [Extreme Low Light Quality] FULL Haunted Mansion Ride-Through 2015 - Disneyland (2015). https://youtu.be/RXO8rt92BIA

Sources of Insight, *Walt Disney Quotes* (accessed 2019). http://sourcesofinsight.com/walt-disney-quotes/

Sternberg, Robert J. and Lubart, Todd I. "The Concept of Creativity: Prospects and Paradigms" in the *Handbook of Creativity* (1999). Cambridge University Press, U.S.

Surrell, Jason. *The Haunted Mansion: From the Magic Kingdom to the Movies* (2003). Disney Editions, New York.

Surrell, Jason. *The Haunted Mansion: Imagineering a Disney Classic* (2015). Disney Editions, New York.

The Haunted Mansion Wiki. Pet Cemetery (accessed 2018). http://hauntedmansion.wikia.com/wiki/Pet_Cemetery

Torrance, E. Paul. *The Search for Satori and Creativity* (1979). The Creative Education Foundation and Creative Synergetic Associates, Buffalo, New York.

Tvshow1701. *The Story and Song from The HAUNTED MANSION LP* (2012). https://youtu.be/5UeS0cjzIj0

Vault Disney. *HAUNTED MANSION - Visited By Kurt Russell & The Osmonds* (2008). https://youtu.be/yEPdN__ZmYo

"Walt Disney Quotes." BrainyQuote.com. BrainyMedia Inc, 2019. 26 April 2019. https://www.brainyquote.com/quotes/walt_disney_131640

Ward, Thomas B., Smith, Steven M. and Finke, Ronald A. "Creative Cognition" in the *Handbook of Creativity* (1999). Cambridge University Press, U.S.

Weisberg, Robert W. "Creativity and Knowledge: A Challenge to Theories" in the *Handbook of Creativity* (1999). Cambridge University Press, U.S.

Williams, Pat and Denney, Jim. *How to be Like Walt: Capturing the Disney Magic Every Day of Your Life* (2004). Health Communications, Inc., Deerfield, FL.

Wright, Alex and the Imagineers. *The Imagineering Field Guide to Disneyland: An Imagineer's-Eye Tour* (2008). Disney Editions, New York.

About the Author

Shad Engkilterra has been a Disney fan for all of his life. There was a point when he realized that women weren't really interested in Disney fans, so he tried to hide his love of all things Disney. On a second date, the woman he was with asked him how long he had been a Disney fan. Shad was confused. How did she know. She pointed out all of the things she noticed including his license plate frame. Shad wasn't very good at hiding his Disney obsession, and from that moment on, decided to embrace it.

Shad has been to Disneyland 50 times – the 50th serving as research for this book. He worked at Walt Disney World as a custodian in 2012 as part of the College Program. His home resorts were Saratoga Springs and Old Key West, which had the best music of any of the resorts he worked at. Shad covered the opening of Euro Disneyland (now called Disneyland Paris) for the Albany-Democrat Herald and had an annual pass to the park while he was in college in Germany.

Shad received his Master's of Creativity and Innovation from Malta University's Edward de Bono Institute. While in Malta, he became an archery instructor and visited Disneyland Paris once with his mom. Shad also has a Bachelor's in German from Linfield College, and an Associate's in Communication from Salt Lake Community College. "The Haunted Mansion Is Creativity" is Shad's 9th book.

www.ingramcontent.com/pod-product-compliance
Lightning Source LLC
Chambersburg PA
CBHW031136090426
42738CB00008B/1109